Sarbanes-Oxley
for Small Businesses

Sarbanes-Oxley for Small Businesses

Leveraging
Compliance for
Maximum Advantage

PEGGY M. JACKSON, DPA, CPCU

WILEY

John Wiley & Sons, Inc.

Copyright © 2006 by John Wiley & Sons, Inc. All rights reserved.

Published by John Wiley & Sons, Inc., Hoboken, New Jersey.

Published simultaneously in Canada.

For general information on our other products and services, or technical support, please contact our Customer Care Department within the United States at 800–762–2974, outside the United States at 317–572–3993, or fax 317–572–4002.

Wiley also publishes its books in a variety of electronic formats. Some content that appears in print may not be available in electronic books.

For more information about Wiley products, visit our Web site at www.wiley.com.

Library of Congress Cataloging-in-Publication Data

Jackson, Peggy M.
  Sarbanes-Oxley for small businesses : leveraging compliance for maximum advantage / Peggy M. Jackson.
    p. cm.
  Includes bibliographical references and index.
  ISBN-13: 978–0-471–99825–9 (cloth)
  ISBN-10: 0–471–99825–7 (cloth)
    1. Small business—United States—Finance—Management. 2. United States. Sarbanes-Oxley Act of 2002. 3. Accounting—Standards—United States. 4. Auditing, Internal—Standards—United States. I. Title.
  HG4027.7.J33 2006
  657'.9042—dc22   2006005665

Printed in the United States of America

10 9 8 7 6 5 4 3 2 1

I am dedicating this book to my colleagues in the San Francisco Chamber of Commerce Fall 2005 Tuesday evening Business Alliance group. These wonderful people have been tremendously supportive of my work and I am very grateful for all of their help.

Andre Angelantoni

Steven Boullianne

Megan Brenk

Sterling Burnett

Joe DeLucchi

Greg Golden

Courtney Jones

Matthew Kabak, Esq.

Oonagh Kavanagh

Claire Koffel

Meehyun Kim Kurtzman

America Michael

Nicholas Paleologos

Stacey Poole, Esq.

Agnes Puerzer

Bart Saling

Jamie Stern

Juancho Vitangcol

Michael Wolfe

Omar Zayat

Contents

Preface

Not too long ago, while having coffee with a business colleague, he made the comment that small business owners, whose days are typically filled with one crisis after another, feel overwhelmed by the scope of Sarbanes-Oxley legislation. These businesspeople often find themselves putting out fires throughout their business day, caused by workers who don't show up, customers who have problems with their orders, endless phone calls, and other problems that need immediate resolution. In the face of such stress, and if seen just as a regulatory burden, Sarbanes-Oxley compliance can be a source of frustration for business owners with already too much on their plate.

The focus of this book, then, is to facilitate a better and "healthier" understanding of what Sarbanes-Oxley has to offer small businesses. To that end, the book not only covers the compliance imperatives that Sarbanes-Oxley requires of small businesses, but it also shows how businesses can reap large rewards if they enter into this process with their eyes wide open. For example, many small businesses launch their operations without really establishing a solid infrastructure. Thus, their businesses may grow, but in a haphazard manner. IT systems don't "talk" to each other, policies and procedures are not in place to manage internal controls, and the daily operation of the business is constantly in crisis mode. It doesn't have to be that way! Sarbanes-Oxley requirements (there are only two for small businesses) and best practices can help small business owners strengthen their internal controls; organize their documents; and keep their companies safe by encouraging early reporting of waste, fraud, and abuse.

As an additional aid, I have designed a Blueprint model that small businesses can use to help streamline the implementation of these requirements and best practices. Using these tools, Sarbanes-Oxley legislation can help to lower costs for small businesses and enable them to become more competitive.

Peggy M. Jackson
August 2006

Acknowledgments

I would like to thank my editor, Tim Burgard, for his assistance and support. One of the most enjoyable aspects of writing is being able to work with the wonderful Wiley editorial staff.

Tyler Boyd of ADP's Small Business Services, and one of my colleagues in the San Francisco Center City BNI group, was very helpful in providing guidance for my discussion of working with professionals.

I would also like to acknowledge the support and encouragement that I receive from friends, family, and colleagues. Paul, Rick, Jan, and Gemma keep things in humorous perspective. I am also grateful for the support from my colleagues in the San Francisco Junior League. You have been steadfast in cheering me on and are a constant source of inspiration.

PMJ

CHAPTER 1

History and Legislative Background of the Sarbanes-Oxley Act of 2002

INTRODUCTION

As a small business owner, on a daily basis you have to deal with multiple crises that demand your attention and require you to juggle resources. You have to cope with regulations, and may feel there is no time left over to ponder the finer details of legislation that seems to apply only to *Fortune* 500 companies. The truth of the matter is that, in spite of the countless problems that you deal with every day, it's essential for you to understand how Sarbanes–Oxley legislation affects your company. The good news is that by leveraging these requirements (there are only two that apply to private companies) and best practices, you can save your company money, lower overhead costs, and improve sales.

BACKGROUND: THE ECONOMIC HISTORY BEHIND SARBANES-OXLEY LEGISLATION

The Sarbanes-Oxley Act (SOX) is the latest in a long progression of regulatory reform aimed at rectifying corporate misdeeds. SOX has its roots in the Great Depression, which began in 1929 and lasted more than a decade and distinguished itself as one of the deepest economic slumps to ever affect the United States, Europe, and other industrialized countries.

Although the actual causes of the Great Depression are still intensely debated, some of the factors believed to have contributed to it in the United States were: the mass stock speculation that occurred during the 1920s; a general imbalance of purchasing power and wealth, in that a large percentage of the population was poor while a small percentage was very wealthy; the laissez-faire economic philosophy adhered to by Presidents Warren Harding (1920–1923), Calvin Coolidge (1923–1928), and Herbert Hoover (1929–1933); and the catastrophic nosedive of stock prices on the New York Stock Exchange (NYSE) on October 29, 1929. On that day, known as "Black Tuesday," the U.S. stock market crashed, and the value of stock steeply plummeted. Black Tuesday was one of the worst trading days in the history of the stock market. Not only did stock prices collapse, but most of the financial gains of the previous year were wiped out within the first few hours of the market's opening. And because most Americans viewed the stock market as the chief indicator of the health of the economy, the 1929 crash also destroyed public confidence in both the stock market and in the U.S. economy.

Stock value continued to fall for approximately three years, until late 1932. By that time, stocks had lost 80 percent of their value from 1929. Individual investors suffered devastating losses and, overnight, large fortunes were wiped out. Many banks and other financial institutions, particularly those holding a large portion of stocks in their portfolios, also suffered severe losses in assets and, by 1933, 11,000 of the 25,000 banks in the United States had failed. In part, the 1929 crash was blamed on wildly inflated stock prices; poor monetary policies imposed by the Federal Reserves Board; fraud, concealed, or misleading financial information; the rampant buying of stock on margin; and inadequate controls on trading in the U.S. market. In 1932, newly elected President Franklin D. Roosevelt and Congress sought to regulate the market by imposing controls on trading, and requiring organizations that were offering securities for public sale to provide financial and other significant information about the securities being offered.

Two important pieces of legislation emerged from this turbulent time. The first, the Securities Act of 1933—frequently referred to as the "Truth in Securities" law—focused on, one, assuring that investors be fully informed about the financial aspects of securities being offered for sale and, two, on prohibiting deceit, misrepresentations, and other fraud in securities transactions. The second piece of legislation was the Securities Exchange Act of 1934, which created the Securities and Exchange Commission (SEC) and gave it the power to regulate many aspects of the securities industry. The act also provided the SEC with the authority to require periodic reporting of financial information by organizations that offered publicly traded securities, and gave the commission the power to register, regulate, and oversee brokerage firms, transfer agents, and the stock exchanges. The two acts gave the SEC the power to:

- Regulate and register stock exchanges as well as all securities listed on an exchange.
- Regulate investment advisors and all dealers and brokers who are members of an organized exchange.
- Require that audited and current financial reports be filed.
- Set accounting standards.
- Prohibit all forms of stock price manipulation, such as insider trading.

The availability of properly audited and current financial reports enables investors to make informed and rational choices about whether to invest in a particular company. The audited financial reports are available from the organizations selling the securities in their stockholders' annual reports.

Report of the National Commission on Fraudulent Financial Reporting

The impetus for Sarbanes-Oxley legislation can trace its roots to long before the corporate misdeeds of Enron. Corporate misbehavior never seems to go out of style, and evidence of it reemerged in the late 1980s, following a series of high-profile corporate offenses. The National Commission on Fraudulent Financial Reporting, also known as the Treadway Commission (reflecting the name of its first chairperson,

James C. Treadway, Jr.), took the lead in examining the factors that led to fraudulent behavior and making recommendations to reduce the potential for future fraud.

The 1980s were also a time of corporate scandal, the scope of which pales in comparison to today's corporate catastrophes. Corporate takeovers in the 1980s cost many people their jobs, but the scale of those problems cannot compare to the corporate implosion of Enron, which resulted in tens of thousands of people losing their jobs and their life savings. The Commission of Sponsoring Organizations (COSO), a voluntary private sector organization, was formed in 1985 to sponsor the aforementioned National Commission on Fraudulent Financial Reporting (the "Treadway Commission"), which was jointly supported by the American Accounting Association (AAA), the American Institute of Certified Public Accountants (AICPA), Financial Executives International (FEI), the Institute of Internal Auditors (IIA), and the National Association of Accountants. The purpose of the Commission was to identify the factors that can lead to fraudulent financial reporting and to develop recommendations to address these factors. Independent of each of its supporting organizations, it consisted of representatives from industry, public accounting, investment firms, and the New York Stock Exchange.

In 1987, the Commission published its findings in the *Report of the National Commission on Fraudulent Financial Reporting* (COSO, 1987). The report indicated that fraud occurs as "the result of certain environmental, institutional, or individual forces and opportunities." Examples of these forces include:

- Weak or nonexistent internal controls
- Weak ethical climate
- Desire to earn a higher price from a stock or debt offering
- Attempts to meet shareholder expectations
- Desire to postpone dealing with financial difficulties
- Personal gain, such as additional compensation, promotion, or escape from penalty for poor performance

- Unrealistic budget pressures, particularly for short-term results
- Absence of a board of directors or audit committee to properly oversee the financial reporting process
- Ineffective internal audit employee

Many of the findings and recommendations from the Commission were incorporated into SOX, and it was the *Report of the National Commission on Fraudulent Financial Reporting,* plus additional COSO publications, that were major factors driving the swift passage of SOX.

Internal Controls Integrated Framework

As part of their work in identifying the factors that contributed to corporate fraud, the members of the Commission also designed a model for corporations to use to address the remedies in a coherent fashion. In 1992, COSO published the "Internal Controls–Integrated Framework" (the "Framework) for developing an effective internal control system. The Framework provides direction to any business that wishes to establish an effective internal control system. Specifically, it breaks effective internal control into five interrelated components: control environment, risk assessment, control activities, information/communication, and monitoring.

Although the Sarbanes-Oxley Act of 2002 was passed primarily in response to wrongdoing and fiscal mismanagement in public companies, one of its effects has been to promote greater accountability within the private sector, regardless of the size of the company and regardless of whether the company is public or private.

FAST-FORWARD TO THE TWENTY-FIRST CENTURY: SOX IS PASSED

The Sarbanes-Oxley Act of 2002—formally, the Public Company Accounting Reform and Investor Protection Act of 2002 (P.L. 107–204)—was signed into law by President George W. Bush on July 30,

2002. SOX has been described as the "most far-reaching reforms of American business practices since the time of Franklin Delano Roosevelt" (Office of the Press Secretary, July 30, 2002). Only the Securities Act of 1933 and the Securities Exchange Act of 1934 rival SOX in its effects on public accounting, financial disclosure, and corporate governance. The act significantly broadens the authority and resources of the SEC to monitor and regulate the securities market, and imposes stiff penalties for noncompliance. In essence, the legislation complements the aim of the Securities Act of 1933 to provide "truth in securities" by improving the quality of financial reporting, independent audits, corporate accountability, and accounting services for public companies.

Compared to other legislative acts passed by Congress, SOX became law relatively quickly. On February 14, 2002, House Representative Michael G. Oxley (R-OH), the chairperson of the House Committee on Financial Services, introduced H.R. 3763 (H.R. 3763, 2002). The purpose of the proposed legislation was "to protect investors by improving the accuracy and reliability of corporate disclosures made pursuant to the securities laws, and for other purposes" (H.R. 3763, 2002). The bill had 30 House cosponsors, and was passed by the House on April 24, 2002, by a vote of 334 to 90.

On June 25, 2002, Senator Paul S. Sarbanes (D-Maryland), the chairperson of the Senate Committee on Banking, Housing, and Urban Affairs, introduced S. 2673 (S. 2673, 2002). The purpose of this proposed legislation was "to improve quality and transparency in financial reporting and independent audits and accounting services for public companies, to create a Public Company Accounting Oversight Board, to enhance the standard setting process for accounting practices, to strengthen the independence of firms that audit public companies, to increase corporate responsibility and the usefulness of corporate financial disclosure, to protect the objectivity and independence of securities analysts, to improve Securities and Exchange Commission resources and oversight, and for other purposes" (S. 2673, 2002). The Senate passed the bill on July 15, 2002, by a vote of 97 to 0.

Both the Senate and the House passed, almost unanimously, the Conference Committee Report (H.R. Rep. No. 107–610, 2002) that resolved the differences between the two bills: 423 to 3 in the House and 99 to 0 in the Senate. On July 30, 2002, President George W. Bush signed the bill, and the sweeping reforms required by the act became public law (P.L. 107–204, 2002).

FACTORS DRIVING THE SWIFT PASSAGE OF SOX

Corporate Scandals

One of the drivers of the swift passage of the legislation was the tidal wave of corporate and accounting scandals that rocked the U.S. financial markets in 2000, 2001, and 2002. The SEC, the Department of Justice, the Federal Energy Regulatory Commission, the Federal Bureau of Investigation, and the U.S. Attorney Offices in New York, Denver, and Houston were all investigating a number of publicly held companies for falsifying financial statements, using questionable accounting procedures, mismanaging assets, or otherwise misleading their shareholders and the public about their financial standing.

Here are some examples of allegations of corporate fraudulent behavior:

- Adelphia Communications gave the founding Rigas family and other executives $3.1 billion in off-the-books loans, and hid the loans.
- Bristol-Myers Squibb inflated its 2001 revenues by forcing wholesalers to accept more inventory than needed.
- Enron boosted profits and hid debts by improperly using off-the-books partnerships, manipulated the California and Texas energy markets, and bribed foreign governments to win contracts abroad.
- Global Crossing inflated revenues by engaging in network capacity "swaps" with other carriers and shredded documents related to accounting practices.
- Halliburton recorded $100 million in annual construction cost overruns before clients had agreed to pay for them.

- ImClone CEO Sam Waksal engaged in insider training and improperly used ImClone assets as collateral for a personal bank loan of $44 million.

- WorldCom recorded $3.8 billion in operating expenses as capital expenses and gave founder Bernard Ebbers $400 million in off-the-books loans.

Enron

For several years, the Enron Corporation, an energy company, participated in a number of partnership transactions that lost the organization a substantial amount of money. In 2001, Enron reported that it had failed to follow generally accepted accounting practices (GAAP) in its financial statements for 1997 through 2001 by excluding these unprofitable transactions. In these fallacious financial statements, the organization reported large profits when, in fact, it had lost a total of $586 million during those years. Neither internal nor external controls detected the financial losses disguised as profits. The revelation of the misleading financial reporting led to a collapse in the price of Enron stock: it fell from $83 per share in December 2000 to less than $1 per share in December 2001. Nevertheless, some of Enron's managers made millions of dollars by selling their company stock before its price plummeted. In stark contrast, other investors experienced substantial losses, including Enron employees who had invested a large portion of their retirement portfolios in Enron stock.

Several aspects of the scandal made Enron's behavior seem particularly egregious. The first was the sheer volume of losses. Thousands of employees, many who had worked for decades at Enron, lost their jobs. Many also saw their life savings dissipated, as they were prohibited from selling off their Enron stock when the value of the stock went into freefall. They had been given routine assurances that all was well by senior managers—who are currently facing prosecution.

Millions of people who were not Enron employees also were adversely affected by the scandal. In the months immediately preceding Enron's implosion, the company, along with other power suppliers, manipulated the supply of electric power to states such as California, causing a series of rolling blackouts throughout the summer of 2002. Electricity rates soured, and the governor of California was eventually recalled because of his inadequate response to the manipulation of the state's electric power supply by Enron and others. Media attention on Enron at this time was near constant, and the public was demanding immediate action. Still, it took until January 2006 for the trials of Enron's founder and former Chairman, Kenneth Lay, and former CEO, Jeffrey Skilling, to commence.

WorldCom

In 2002, WorldCom, Inc., a prominent telecommunications company, admitted that it had failed to report more than $7 billion in expenses over five quarterly periods. Its financial statements indicated that WorldCom had been profitable over those quarters, when the company had actually lost $1.2 billion. WorldCom's market worth plunged from $200 billion to only $10 billion in July, when the company filed for Chapter 11 bankruptcy, raising concerns among its investors, creditors, and telecommunication customers.

Enron and WorldCom were not the only companies that released questionable financial statements during this period. Other firms involved in corporate and accounting scandals included Tyco, Adelphia Communications, Xerox, and Global Crossing. These incidents, understandably, shook the public confidence in the capital markets and in the integrity of corporate financial statements. In response to public outrage and the downward spiral in the stock market, the 107th Congress passed the Public Company Accounting Reform and Investor Protection Act, which was signed into law by President George W. Bush on July 30, 2002.

Auditor Scandals

Certified public accounting firms also had their share of high-profile scandals, prompted by the release of false or misleading financial information in connection with high-profile scandals such Enron. Public companies registered with the SEC are required to have their financial statements audited by an external auditor. When an auditor from a public accounting firm examines the financial statements of public companies and gives an unqualified opinion regarding those statements, the shareholders and the public should have increased assurance that the statements were prepared in accordance with GAAP, that GAAP was applied on a consistent basis, and that the statements included all of the information necessary to fairly present the company's financial standing. Based on these requirements, how, then, were public companies able to produce such misleading financial statements?

There are a number of reasons why the auditor's opinion does not necessarily represent the accurate condition of the financial statements. In some cases, auditors simply make errors. In other cases, however, an auditor's opinion may be biased, or the auditor may have a financial incentive to misrepresent the accuracy of the financial statements. If, for example, the firm performing the audit is also receiving substantial compensation for providing consulting, tax work, or other services, the accounting firm has a financial incentive to maintain a good relationship with the company being audited. The desire to maintain the relationship—and the compensation—may bias the auditor to report a more positive financial position than actually exists. Biased auditor reports can also occur when the relationship between management of the company being audited and the auditor is too "cozy"; that is, the loyalty of the auditor may lie with management, rather than with the shareholders; thus, the auditor's evaluation of the statements may be swayed by that loyalty.

Arthur Andersen LLP and Enron

For several years, Enron participated in a number of partnership transactions that lost the company a substantial amount of money. In 2001, Enron reported that it had failed to follow GAAP in its financial statements for 1997 through 2001 by excluding these unprofitable transactions. In these misleading financial statements, the organization reported large profits when, in fact, it had lost a total of $586 million during those years. Neither internal nor external controls detected the financial losses disguised as profits. The revelation of this fallacious reporting led to a collapse in the price of Enron stock, which, as stated previously, fell dramatically, from $83 per share in December 2000 to less than $1 per share in December 2001. In spite of this, as also noted earlier, some of Enron's managers made millions of dollars by selling their company stock before its price plummeted, whereas other investors experienced substantial losses, including Enron employees who had invested a large portion of their retirement portfolios in Enron stock (*Securities and Exchange Commission v. Timothy A. DeSpain*, 2005; *Securities and Exchange Commission v. Richard A. Causey, Jeffery K. Skilling and Kenneth L. Lay*, 2004).

The certified public accounting firm of Arthur Andersen LLP, which had been one of the largest accounting firms in the world, served as Enron's auditor during the years of these erroneous statements were released. Allegedly, the firm "overlooked" Enron's questionable accounting practices because it was making a large amount of money for providing Enron with consulting services and did not want to lose this lucrative client.

Arthur Andersen was indicted by the U.S. Department of Justice, and, in June 2002, a jury convicted the firm of obstructing justice by shredding Enron-related documents requested by the SEC. U.S. District Judge Melinda Harmon sentenced the firm to a $500 billion fine and five years' probation. The conviction also essentially decimated the formerly powerful "Big Five" firm—it lost most of its clients.

Subsequently, however, the firm got a lucky break, courtesy of a judicial mishap. Though the 5th U.S. Circuit Court of Appeals affirmed the jury verdict, on May 31, 2005, the U.S. Supreme Court overturned the obstruction-of-justice conviction. According to Supreme Court justices, the conviction was improper because the instructions given jurors during the trial were too broad and vague, hence they were unable to correctly determine whether the company actually committed the crime. Thus, the reversal of the firm's criminal conviction was based entirely on a trial technicality (*Arthur Anderson LLP v. United States*, 2005).

Certainly, the relationship between Enron and Arthur Andersen LLP is a dramatic example of failure in the auditing process, but the auditing practices and relationships with clients of a number of other accounting firms also came under fire. Examples include Deloitte Touche and Adelphia, Ernst & Young and AOL, KPMG and Xerox, and PricewaterhouseCoopers and Bristol-Myers Squibb.

RESPONSE OF PRESIDENT BUSH
AND THE 107TH CONGRESS

As more and more scandals came to light, understandably, the public confidence in the capital markets and in the integrity of corporate financial statements was badly shaken. To both assuage public dissatisfaction and to halt the downward plummet in the stock market, President George W. Bush and the 107th Congress presented a plan to upgrade public expectations of corporate responsibility.

On March 7, 2002, the President announced his Ten-Point Plan to Improve Corporate Responsibility and Protect America's Shareholders, based on three core principles: information accuracy and accessibility, management accountability, and auditor independence. The points of the plan were:

- Each investor should have quarterly access to the information needed to judge a firm's financial performance, condition, and risks.

- Each investor should have prompt access to critical information.

- CEOs should personally vouch for the veracity, timeliness, and fairness of their companies' public disclosures, including their financial statements.

- CEOs or other officers should not be allowed to profit from erroneous financial statements.

- CEOs or other officers who clearly abuse their power should lose their right to serve in any corporate leadership positions.

- Corporate leaders should be required to tell the public promptly whenever they buy or sell company stock for personal gain.

- Investors should have complete confidence in the independence and integrity of companies' auditors.

- An independent regulatory board should ensure that the accounting profession is held to the highest ethical standards.

- The authors of accounting standards must be responsive to the needs of investors.

- Firms' accounting systems should be compared with best practices, not simply against minimum standards.

On July 9, 2002, President Bush issued Executive Order 1371, which established the Corporate Fraud Task Force within the Department of Justice. Former Deputy Attorney General Larry Thompson led the task force, which included U.S. attorneys, the FBI, and the SEC, and was charged with overseeing the investigation and prosecution of financial fraud, accounting fraud, and other corporate criminal activity; and with providing enhanced interagency coordination of regulatory and criminal investigations. He explained the goal of the president's Corporate Fraud Task Force as follows: "As we establish with ever increasing certainty the prospect that corporate criminals will lose both their fortunes and their liberty, we will have gone a long way to restoring the integrity of the market and the confidence of the nation" (Office of the Press Secretary, 2002).

The response of Congress was the relatively quick passage of SOX, a substantial piece of legislation. It took less than six months (from February 14 to July 15) for both chambers of Congress to pass the bill and to send it to President Bush for signature, which, as noted previously, he did on July 30, 2002.

COMPONENTS OF SOX AFFECTING SMALL BUSINESSES

Many would agree that SOX is the single most important piece of legislation affecting corporate governance, financial disclosure, and public accounting since the passage of the Securities Act of 1933 and the Securities Exchange Act of 1934. SOX contains sweeping reforms for issuers of publicly traded securities, auditors, corporate board members, and lawyers. It adopts new provisions intended to deter and punish corporate and accounting fraud and corruption, and imposes stiff penalties for noncompliance. In essence, SOX seeks to protect the interest of shareholders and employees by improving the overall quality of financial reporting, independent audits, corporate accountability, and accounting services for public companies.

Several sections of the law address requirements and/or best practices for small businesses. At this point in time only whistleblower protection and document preservation are specific requirements for all organizations, including private companies. However, indications are that more requirements will be imposed on private companies as fraud continues to occur across all sectors.

Title II

Title II of SOX details the rules for establishing the independence of the auditor from the company being audited. It defines which additional services the auditing firm may and may not provide, defines and prohibits conflicts of interest between auditors and the audited company, requires that the audited firm rotate its auditors on a regular basis, and requires the audit committee of the audited company to be responsible for the oversight of its auditors. Although auditor independence is mandatory for publicly traded firms, small businesses also can benefit from the best practice of auditor independence.

Titles III and IV

Titles III and IV of SOX detail the responsibilities and roles to be played by the audited company in regard to the audit and reports. For example, the principal executive and financial officers of the company are directly responsible for certifying that the information in the annual or quarterly reports required by the SEC Act of 1934 is accurate, complete, and fairly presented. In addition, rules are included to address insider trading and the professional responsibility of attorneys to report violations of securities law or breech of fiduciary duty. Titles III and IV also outline the disclosure requirements of relevant financial information, such as off-balance-sheet arrangements and relationships.

Titles VIII, IX, X, and XI

Titles VIII, IX, X, and XI outline the penalties for securities fraud and document destruction or alteration; create whistleblower protection for employee informants; and establish corporate responsibility for financial reports.

Title VIII, also referred to as the Corporate and Criminal Fraud Accountability Act of 2002, creates criminal penalties for fraud and document destruction, provides protection for whistleblowers who provide evidence of fraud, specifies that debts incurred in violation of securities fraud laws are nondischargeable (Section 803), extends the statute of limitations on securities fraud claims, and creates a new crime for defrauding shareholders of publicly traded companies (Section 807).

Document destruction: Section 802 amends the federal obstruction-of-justice statute. It is now a felony to "knowingly" destroy, conceal, cover up, add to, or falsify documents or records in order to impede or obstruct any federal investigation or bankruptcy proceeding. Destruction of documents with intent to obstruct a federal investigation was already a criminal offense under the existing statute, but it applied only to ongoing investigations. The new offense also covers contemplated investigations and provides for the imposition of fines, imprisonment for up to 20 years, or both, for the violation of the statute.

Preservation of audit materials: Auditors can also be charged with a felony if they fail to retain all audit and review work papers and materials for a period of five years from the end of the fiscal year in which the audit was conducted. Section 802 provides for the imposition of fines, imprisonment for up to 10 years, or both, for the violation of the statute.

Whistleblower protection: Under Section 806, employees of public companies and accounting firms who disclose private company or firm information as evidence of accounting or auditing violations or fraud to a supervisor, federal regulator, law enforcement agency, or member of Congress are extended whistleblower protection. Under whistleblower protection, it is unlawful for the employer to discriminate against the employee in any manner if that employee engaged in the protected activity. Discrimination includes actions such as discharge, demotion, suspension, threats or harassment, blacklisting, and disciplinary actions. Under this section, whistleblowers are granted a remedy of special damages and attorney's fees. The Public Company Accounting Oversight Board (PCAOB) has established the Center for Enforcement Tips, Complaints, and Other Information to provide employees with an easy avenue for submitting evidence to the PCAOAB (Public Company Accounting Oversight Board, 2003).

Title IX states that each periodic report containing financial statements filed with the SEC must be accompanied by a written statement by the issuer's CEO and CFO certifying that the report fully complies with the 1934 Act and that information contained in the periodic report "fairly presents, in all material respects, the financial condition and results of operations of the issuer." Publicly traded companies are required to have their CEO and/or CFO attest, under penalty of law, that their financials are accurate. Small business CEOs and CFOs should incorporate the best practice of ensuring that all financials are accurate and fairly depict the financial condition of the company.

NEXT STEPS

Sarbanes-Oxley legislation was not the first attempt to deal with corporate malfeasance. Shareholder activism and public outrage over the loss of tens of thousands of jobs and millions of dollars in individual investments by employees of Enron, WorldCom, and other corporations ensured that the provisions of this law would have "teeth." The law's expectations of transparency and accountability also offer the means by which small businesses can leverage their compliance and the best practices to reduce costs and improve competitive positioning.

In Chapter 2 we will examine the reasons why small businesses should care about Sarbanes-Oxley compliance, whose practices are now considered the gold standard in business management.

Why Should Small Businesses Care about SOX?

Consider the following example, based on a real-life case: A small business owner hired his brother-in-law, who has had an accounting background, to run the books for his business. The business grew steadily over the years, but still functioned with the same "Mom and Pop" mindset and profile that was used to launch the venture years ago. Early on, the brother-in-law's bookkeeping and accounting knowledge came in handy for a business owner who has to watch every dime. His family connections made the brother-in-law even more valuable, as the owner was very leery of allowing any outsiders to handle the company's books. The brother-in-law did everything—bookkeeping, taxes, and even annual audits of the company. No one else ever touched the books.

All went well until the day that the owner received a notification from the IRS that his latest tax return is to be audited. As the owner began to examine the financial records of the business, he was horrified to discover that his brother-in-law, this trusted family member, had embezzled approximately $7 million over the past decade. In retrospect, he realized there were earlier warning signals. Several months earlier, the owner had received a letter from the insurance company that wrote his business insurance stating that the company would not renew his crime policy, due to expire in three months, because of the owner's refusal to allow anyone other than his brother-in-law to handle the books or sign checks. The company's insurance broker was equally shocked when this long-time client filed a claim with the insurance provider. Although the claim will probably be paid by the insurance carrier because the current policy was still active, placing the company with a new insurer will be very difficult. Even if another insurer is willing to take the company, the premium they will have to pay will be significantly higher.

FIVE REASONS WHY SMALL BUSINESSES SHOULD CARE ABOUT SOX

Many small business owners never understand the importance of establishing a strong infrastructure at the launch of their companies: to accommodate growth. Sarbanes-Oxley requirements and best practices can give small business owners the essential framework to both embrace and sustain growth throughout the lifetime of their businesses. SOX legislation presents value and opportunity for small businesses in creating sustainable infrastructures, and its compliance and best practices are rapidly becoming the benchmark for evaluating the operational risk that a company presents.

Here are five reasons why small businesspeople should care, and be enthused, about SOX.

1. The current trend is toward holding CFOs or other senior management criminally liable for veracity of financials and tax returns.

2. Banks that are publicly traded entities prefer to have clients who are in compliance with SOX.

3. Best practices that emerge with SOX compliance are becoming the gold standard for management.

4. Boards are being held more accountable.

5. Sources of capital (VC firms) will demand transparency. Being in compliance offers small companies a competitive advantage

   Bonus Reason: Compliance with SOX and implementation of best practices can save your firm money, and position your small business to increase sales and improve operational efficiency.

Let's examine each of these reasons more closely.

CFOs or Other Senior Management Will Be Criminally Liable

This trend, to hold senior management liable for the veracity of financials and tax returns, is fully in place. Small publicly traded firms are often the targets of SEC enforcement, and the trend is to hold all businesses—public, private, and nonprofit—accountable in a similar fashion.

Banks Prefer Clients in Compliance with SOX

The risk profile of a company is now being measured in terms of the quality of its SOX compliance and integration of best practices. Financial institutions such as banks, particularly those that are publicly traded entities, are expected to ensure that their clients are in compliance with SOX. Small businesses that have integrated SOX requirements and best practices are, therefore, much better positioned to negotiate favorable interest rates and other terms. Insurance underwriters are more willing to accept a new client and negotiate competitive premium packages. Companies that have taken steps to come into SOX compliance and implement its best practices are considered to be better risks.

SOX Best Practices Are Becoming the Gold Standard for Business Management

Implementing best practices can serve to save a business owner time and money, particularly if there is the possibility that the company may want to eventually go public. Before a company can launch an IPO, the firm will be required to prove that it is in full compliance with every provision of Sarbanes-Oxley legislation. The COSO Integrated Framework, mentioned in Chapter 1, established a model for adaptation of best practices. Although the framework is designed for publicly traded firms, the COSO model can easily be scaled down to suit the needs of small businesses and expanded as the business grows.

Corporate Boards Are Being Held More Accountable

In 2005, New York Attorney General Eliott Spitzer assessed a hefty fine on several board members of WorldCom, which they were required to pay out of their personal funds (*San Francisco Chronicle*, January 5, 2005, http://www.sfgate.com/chronicle/). Although not every small business has a board, many small companies do have boards often comprised of members of the family who own the business. The interaction of family members within a business framework presents a layer of particularly thorny governance issues that can be dealt with more efficiently by implementation of SOX requirements and best practices. Compliance with legal requirements and standards also can serve to neutralize family squabbles.

Sources of Capital Will Demand Transparency

Being in compliance offers your company a competitive advantage. The dot-com boom and subsequent bust was a tough lesson for venture capitalists. The result is that, today, they are much less willing to underwrite companies that have murky infrastructures and seat-of-the-pants management.

Bonus Reason: Save Money and Improve Competitive Advantage

Compliance with SOX and implementation of best practices can save your firm money and position your small business to increase sales and improve operational efficiency. In addition, SOX compliance can generate greater value from the relationships that your company already has, with its bank, legal counsel, and insurance and IT professionals.

SOX can help your company save money in a number of ways:

- *Get better interest rates.* Interest rates on loans are based on the lender's perception of risk. Being in compliance with SOX requirements and implementing the best practices that emerged from the SOX legislation will help your firm improve its credit rating and demonstrate that is a better credit risk.

- *Get more competitive terms for loans or lines of credit.* As your company adopts SOX requirements and best practices, these efforts could have a positive effect on the firm's credit rating, as noted above.

Additionally, being able to demonstrate that your firm is in compliance could be beneficial in negotiating the terms of a loan or line of credit.

- *Be in a better position to negotiate a more favorable fee from auditors.* Although there has been significant media coverage on the increasing costs of audits, it's important to point out that many of these fee increases have been imposed when the client firms are not in compliance. If you feel that your auditor's fees are too high, bid out the job! Don't settle for less than complete value for your auditing dollar. Consider using smaller accounting firms. Supply information on your firm's compliance practices to prospective auditors and aggressively negotiate the fees.

- *Obtain insurance coverage at more a competitive premium.* Insurance underwriters are highly reluctant to extend coverage to businesses that are not in compliance with SOX. Remember, compliance is today's management gold standard, and underwriters are looking for evidence that your company has taken the initiative to integrate SOX requirements and best practices into your day-to-day operations. Doing so tells the underwriter that you know what you are doing and are serious about managing risk in your business.

- *Create additional value from current company relationships.* Bringing your small business into compliance can be facilitated by discussions with your company's banker, legal counsel, and insurance professional IT professionals. These people should know your business inside out. If they don't, then you need to seriously consider finding advisors who can meet these expectations. Leverage their knowledge of your firm and their professional expertise. They can tell you how to come into compliance in an efficient and cost-effective manner. CPAs can help companies use SOX compliance as a stepping stone to improved decision-making procedures, more efficient processes, and greater confidence in financial reporting. Some of these improvements may help companies offset the high cost of complying with the act (Harrington, 2005). (Chapter 8 explains more fully how to work effectively with these professionals.)

- *Position your company to increase sales.* Let the world know that you are in compliance. Demonstrating that your company is in compliance will position your company to increase sales by:
  - Being an attractive vendor or subcontractor to larger firms.
  - Leveraging SOX compliance as a marketing tool—differentiate your business from that of your competitors by taking action to come into compliance.
  - Retaining current clients by bolstering confidence in your firm's integrity and transparency. Demonstrating compliance will serve to reinforce your firm's value as a vendor.
  - Presenting the business "credentials" that are essential in securing contracts with public sector (governmental) entities.
  - Positioning your company as a more attractive prospect if you want to sell the business. Being able to demonstrate compliance and best practices can serve to secure a higher price from a buyer.

Here's how SOX compliance and best practices can reduce overhead costs:

- *Internal controls are in place to standardize procedures.* Having solid internal controls, policies, and procedures introduces a standardized approach to operations and administration. Good internal controls serve as an active deterrent to fraudulent activities, which can drain your company of money and materials.

- *Files are organized in a more efficient manner.* SOX compliance and best practices help you to establish a more efficient system for managing files, databases, and other forms of information.

- *Whistleblower protection policy encourages early warning of waste, fraud, or abuse.* This SOX requirement is probably the most effective method of detecting waste, fraud, and abuse—if you design a system that encourages reports of waste, fraud, and abuse.

- *IT systems are integrated, or in the process of being integrated, to sustain internal controls.* Developing solid internal controls begins with ensuring that your IT system is designed to meet your company's size and needs. The money you spend to ensure that your IT framework will support the necessary internal controls is a solid investment for your company's growth and sustainability.

SOX Value Proposition: Why Now?

As businesses engage in compliance at higher levels, they "increase the value extracted from processes and key initiatives, regardless of the regulatory and auditing environment" (Jefferson Wells, 2005). The added value of SOX requirements and best practices centers on the review of processes on a companywide basis. Examining processes during compliance forces companies to consider how and why they were doing things. When the processes overlap or are illogical, compliance activities stipulate more efficient methods and the elimination of unnecessary steps. More importantly, SOX compliance activities cause senior managers to think about how their companies are organized (Harrington, 2005).

> "The evaluation process has led to improvements in basic internal controls such as reconciliations and segregation of duties. There were substantial improvements in the control environment that came about as a direct result of the process . . . companies have more confidence in their control structure and are evaluating accounting risks, which should enable investors to have more confidence in the reliability of unaudited data furnished to the securities market" (Hermanson, 2005).

OLD TOOL IN A NEW DIMENSION: COSO INTERNAL CONTROLS-INTEGRATED FRAMEWORK

As noted in Chapter 1, in 1987, the Treadway Commission published its findings in the *Report of the National Commission on Fraudulent Financial Reporting* (COSO, 1987). The report indicated that fraud occurs as "the result of certain environmental, institutional, or individual forces and opportunities" (COSO, 1987). Examples of these forces that are applicable to small businesses include:

- Weak or nonexistent internal controls
- Weak ethical climate
- Desire to postpone dealing with financial difficulties
- Personal gain, such as additional compensation, promotion, escape from penalty for poor performance
- Unrealistic budget pressures, particularly for short-term results
- Absence of a board of directors or audit committee that properly oversees the financial reporting process
- Ineffective internal audit employee

The Internal Controls–Integrated Framework that emerged from this study is a tool for organizing and developing an effective internal control system. It breaks effective internal control into five interrelated components: control environment, risk assessment, control activities, information/communication, and monitoring.

Control Environment

The business owner and senior management establish the organizational-level control environment. They set the tone of the business, which influences how people behave within their day-to-day work environment. Because the owner and managers establish the business culture in terms of how the business is run, the culture, in turn, affects the company's internal controls.

Control environment factors include:

- *Integrity and ethical values.* The owner and managers of the business model the company's integrity and ethical values. If you, as the owner, do not behave in an ethical manner, chances are, your managers and employees will not either.
- *Attention and involvement of board of directors.* Does your company have a board of directors? If so, its members need to be actively involved in setting the tone within the company.

- *Commitment to competence.* The business owner and management need to make a highly visible commitment to competence. This means that mediocrity and incompetence have to be rooted out. This might also mean that some people in the firm either will have to be reprimanded and put on probation, to curb their influence, or, if need be, terminated.

- *Management philosophy and operating style.* SOX requirements and best practices offer you, the business owner, and your management team an opportunity to upgrade your management philosophy and improve your operating style.

- *Adherence to authority and responsibility.* SOX requirements and best practices will make it easy for your company to comply with the law, as well as to step up to the responsibility you have as an owner or senior manager.

A business whose CEO both demonstrates a commitment to ethics and expects the same from others in the organization will have a very different control environment from the business whose CEO sets a tone of deceit and greed. Given the importance of the control environment as a component of the internal control system, it is not surprising that SOX contains provisions regarding a code of ethics, which has emerged as a best practice for small businesses.

Risk Assessment

Every business faces a variety of external and internal risks that can threaten the achievement of its objectives. Risk assessment is the identification of those risks and their potential severity. Once the risks have been identified, the business can take steps to manage, eliminate, or mitigate their effects.

Obviously, before the business can assess and take the necessary steps to manage risks, the company objectives must first be established, both at the organizational level and at the activity or process level. The three broad categories of objectives are: operations, financial reporting, and compliance.

- Operations objectives relate to effectiveness and efficiency of the operations, including performance and financial goals and safeguarding resources against loss.

- Financial reporting objectives pertain to the proper preparation of reliable financial statements, including prevention of fraudulent financial reporting.

- Compliance objectives pertain to meeting the requirements of laws and regulations at the federal, state, and local levels.

Within the three broad categories of objectives, there are multiple levels of subobjectives, each with a narrower focus. For example, within the category of financial reporting are the subobjectives of proper preparation of the balance sheet, proper preparation of the statement of operations, and proper preparation of the statement of cash flows. Within the subobjective of proper preparation of the balance sheet is the sub-subobjective of accurate valuation of assets. At each level, the focus becomes more specific.

The level and type of risk varies among businesses, as each is unique in its design and conformation. For example, a business that has many daily cash transactions might face a more severe risk to operations objectives than a business that rarely has many cash transactions. Or a business that has inadequate staffing in its accounting function might face a more severe risk to financial reporting objectives than a business that has an adequately staffed accounting department and provides extensive training for its employees.

Control Activities

Control activities are the policies, procedures, and processes that help ensure management directives are carried out properly and in a timely manner. They help ensure that necessary actions are taken to address risks to the achievement of the organizational objectives.

Control activities occur throughout the organization, at all levels, and in all functions and cover a diverse range, from approvals, authorizations, verifications, and reconciliations to reviews of operating performance, security of assets, and segregation of duties.

Information and Communication

Pertinent information must be identified, captured, and communicated in a form and time frame that enables the owner, managers, and employees to carry out their responsibilities. Effective communication must occur in a broad sense, flowing down, across, and up the organization. Information, both internal and external, must be effectively communicated to management in a timely manner, to enable the board and senior management to make informed business and reporting decisions.

All personnel must be given a clear message from top management that information and communication responsibilities are to be taken seriously. They must also be given a means of communicating significant information up the corporate ladder.

Monitoring

Internal control systems need to have a monitoring process, one that assesses the quality of the system's performance over time. Monitoring is an ongoing activity, which leads to refinement of the internal control system. It occurs during the ordinary course of operations, and includes regular management and supervisory activities and other actions personnel take in performing their duties that assess the quality of internal control system performance.

The scope and frequency of separate evaluations depend primarily on an assessment of risks and the effectiveness of ongoing monitoring procedures. Internal control deficiencies should be reported up the business hierarch, with serious matters reported immediately to senior management and the board of directors.

In monitoring the internal control system, it must be stressed that it is necessary to evaluate not just the control activities component of the system. The monitoring system itself needs to be evaluated, as do the information and communication component, and the risk assessment component. If the effectiveness of the internal control system is not based on all five of the system's components, the effectiveness rating may be higher or lower than the actual rating.

ROLES WITHIN THE FRAMEWORK

Everyone within the business has his or her role in developing and implementing an internal controls system. The roles of course will vary depending on the level of responsibility and the nature of involvement by the individual. The responsibility of the board of directors is to provide guidance to and oversight of the CEO and senior management, especially through the audit committee. The CEO has the responsibility to "set the tone at the top," which will have an overall effect on integrity and ethics; he or she also must provide leadership to senior management. The senior management team provides leadership to department or unit managers and assigns responsibility for the development and implementation of department or unit-specific internal controls. Managers and supervisory personnel are responsible for executing control policies and procedures at the detail level within their specific unit. Each individual within a unit has the responsibility to be cognizant of proper internal control procedures associated with his or her specific job responsibilities. The importance of the roles of management and the board of directors in the internal control system is reflected in several of the SOX requirements for publicly traded firms.

Although the COSO Internal Controls–Integrated Framework was originally designed for *Fortune* 500 companies, the spirit of this tool serves as the inspiration for the Blueprint for change that will be presented in Chapter 5.

NEXT STEPS

Sarbanes-Oxley requirements and best practices can serve as the framework for improving the overall performance of a small business. Chapters 3 and 4 introduce the specific SOX requirements and the best practices that have emerged from this legislation. As just noted, Chapter 5 will introduce the Blueprint tool that can be used by small businesses to introduce change and organize their activities around SOX compliance and best practices.

CHAPTER 3

What Are the Sarbanes-Oxley Requirements for Small Businesses?

W hich one of these people would be most likely to embezzle or misappropriate your company's funds or assets?

- A single mother, aged 23, whose ex-husband is behind on his child support payments
- A teenager who works part-time during the evenings in your warehouse
- A middle-aged man who is a college graduate, owns his own home, and has children in college

If you answered "c," the middle-aged man, you are correct. Contrary to popular belief, the employees who are more likely to misappropriate company funds or assets tend to be middle-aged men who are college educated.

Two primary factors appear to facilitate fraud in small businesses: (1) the lack of internal controls and (2) the reluctance of coworkers to report the situation. The discussion in this chapter will examine the two provisions of SOX that apply to all companies, regardless of their legal structure.

WHAT ARE SMALL BUSINESSES REQUIRED TO DO UNDER SARBANES-OXLEY?

As noted in Chapter 1, only two of the provisions in SOX apply directly to small businesses. The first is whistleblower protection, which provides safeguards to employees who report suspected fraud or other illegal activities. The second is document preservation, which has two aspects:

- Preservation and archiving of documents for the purpose of timely retrieval
- Prohibition against the destruction or falsification of records or documents

WHISTLEBLOWER PROTECTION

The first SOX obligation that applies to all businesses is the requirement for a documented whistleblower protection policy. SOX requires all businesses, including those considered small, to establish a means to collect, retain, and resolve claims regarding accounting, internal accounting controls, and auditing matters. Furthermore, the system must enable such concerns to be submitted anonymously.

SOX provides significant protections to whistleblowers, and severe penalties to those who retaliate against them. Policies and procedures on whistleblower protection should contain at least the following features:

- A confidential avenue for reporting suspected waste, fraud, and abuse
- A process for thoroughly investigating any reports
- A process for disseminating the findings from the investigation
- Assurances that the employee filing the complaint will not be subjected to termination, firing, or harassment, or miss out on promotion
- Assurances that even if the findings do not support the nature of the complaint, the employee who made the complaint will not face repercussions

All employees should be given a copy of the company's whistle-blower policy; in addition, it should be posted in clear view on the company site. And the contents of the policy should be covered in detail in any orientation or training programs the business offers to its employees (see Exhibit 3.1).

Confidentiality is key to developing a process whereby employees feel safe in reporting waste, fraud, and abuse—or even inferior leadership. One way a confidential reporting system can be established is to use an *ombudsman*; another is to use a *third-party reporting system* that is not connected to the business.

Ombudsmen are trained to resolve problems, and have the special tools needed to address complaints of this nature. But to be effective, an ombudsman needs to be independent of the day-to-day business operations, and the position as ombudsman must be secure—that is, it cannot be terminated for any reason other than failure to perform. Having this type of program in place can go a long way to correcting problems as they arise and to meet the SOX requirements.

The alternative, third-party anonymous hotlines can be a risk-free way for employees to report unethical or illegal activity. With a third-party anonymous hotline, an employee can report questionable activities 24/7. Set up properly, such hotlines can handle a variety of reporting issues, such as:

- Accounting irregularities
- Violations of governmental regulations
- Fraud
- Falsification or destruction of business records
- Possible workplace violence, including threats or menacing behavior
- Discrimination
- Sexual harassment
- Conflicts of interest
- Release of proprietary information, particularly if the information has been removed from the workplace

EXHIBIT 3.1   Fraud Detectors

How SOX Whistleblower Protection Requirement Is a Boon for Small Businesses

Every business owner should run, not walk, to put the SOX whistle-blower protection provision in place! Why? To gain these important benefits:

- *Early detection of fraud or misappropriation.* Detecting fraud or other serious conditions early can save your business tens of thousands—if not millions—of dollars. It's the same reason why health insurance companies will gladly pay for cancer screening tests. Catching the disease in its early stages results in significant savings. Reward your whistleblowers!

- *Open forum for discussion.* Implementing a whistleblower protection policy will give you an opportunity to discuss fraud in a mature and straightforward manner with your employees.

- *Aid to change.* A well-crafted whistleblower protection policy will make it easier for you to change any current interpersonal or business dynamics that are not working effectively and need to be remedied. Furthermore, the enforcement of this policy can serve your business well in the event of any frivolous claims of wrongful termination or harassment.

- *Confidentiality*. The whistleblower policy provides you, the business owner, with a confidential means to receive and, subsequently, investigate reports.

- *Equitability*. A whistleblower protection policy lets everyone in the company know that no one is above the law or entitled to misappropriate money, goods, or other assets of the firm.

By ensuring that your company is in compliance with the whistle-blower protection component of SOX, you are protecting your firm's employees, customers, investors, and other stakeholders.

Importance of Talking about Fraud to Your Management Team and Employees

Studies have shown that many of the cases involving fraud first involve the CEO and/or the CFO (COSO, 1999). In these cases, fraud began, literally, at the top. To curb such behavior, then, means that management has to model the type of ethical behavior they expect from the rest of the staff. Modeling ethical behavior is the most effective method of communicating that SOX compliance and ethical behavior is not just something on paper, but that will be carried out in practice. But before management can talk to their employees about fraud, they need to either augment their current ethical standards or design standards to address common areas of executive fraud. Management and senior executives will need to adopt both a conflict of interest policy and a code of ethics (which will be examined in Chapter 4) to include: prohibitions against loans and gifts to management, stringent procedures for travel claims and management of expense accounts, and transparency in their dealings.

Troublesome areas related to fraud include:

- *Loans, gifts, bonuses, and perks to executives.* Small businesspeople often agree to loans and gifts to executives as incentives or as rewards for performance. Businesses, particularly if there is a corporate board, are under much greater scrutiny in terms of how executive compensation packages are approved. Family-owned businesses typically face additional difficulties, as their business and personal relationships often cross professional boundaries.

- *Expense accounts and travel claims.* Financial misappropriation often is hidden in transactions involving expense accounts and travel claims.

- *Lack of an enforceable conflict of interest policy.* A conflict of interest policy should apply to everyone in the company.

- *Minimal internal controls.* The company must have policies and procedures in place to establish controls on revenue and expenses.

- *Ineffective IT system.* When a company's databases and other software are not integrated or subject to effective security measures, additional opportunities to manipulate data and records become apparent.

At the minimum, these issues should be addressed in the human resources policies of every small business.

Remember, as the owner of a small business, you lead the way in changing your company's culture by adopting ethical practices and setting the example by the decisions you make and actions you take. You cannot expect your employees to change their behavior unless they see that you, yourself, have adopted these same measures as part of your daily operations.

When you discuss fraud with your employees, take care to clearly explain what waste, fraud, and abuse look like and how to report these occurrences. As the owner, you need to be open, honest, and frank about how important it is for employees to report waste, fraud, and abuse. Stress how much you value these reports. You might even consider offering rewards to people who submit these reports.

Understanding Why Individuals Are Reluctant to "Blow the Whistle" On Waste, Fraud, and Abuse

It's common knowledge that, despite federal law prohibiting retaliation, whistleblowing is often viewed as a career-limiting gesture. Whistleblowers are not universally embraced by management in any business—

private, public, small, or large. Too often, whistleblowers discover they get virtually no support from management, even if the financial irregularities they identify are egregious. To their dismay, the fraudulent situation goes unremedied and the wrongdoers are not held accountable. Worse, they then find themselves the victim of retaliatory behavior, which can be subtle—such as social ostracism or moving the person's office to a less desirable location—or more explicit, such as obvious efforts to silence or discredit them.

Sometimes whistleblowers find themselves described as "not team players," or categorized as troublemakers. Management may use tactics such as rumor and innuendo to make the whistleblower look bad, either professionally or personally. Other tactics include the silent treatment by supervisors or colleagues or, as just mentioned, changing the location of the person's office or the type of equipment that is assigned to them. Management's displeasure is intended to be obvious to the whistleblower and to everyone else (Sinclair, 2004).

To ensure this does not happen in your company, you, the business owner, must send a clear message to management and employees that any negative response to a person making a report of waste, fraud, or abuse is unacceptable and will not be tolerated or condoned. Whether management approves of or agrees with the whistleblower's message is irrelevant. The whistleblower protection requirement of SOX is clear about the prohibition against retribution of any kind, including subtle acts. It's important to note that in today's legal environment, management can be held responsible for "punishing" a whistleblower even in subtle ways.

Thus, having an effective whistleblower protection policy is important not only to comply with the SOX legal requirements, but also to provide a mechanism for protecting your small business's integrity and future viability. Management needs to establish a mechanism not only to protect whistleblowers, but to *encourage* reporting of waste, fraud, or abuse. The sooner that management and senior executives know about a potential problem, the sooner the problem can be handled. Therefore, you should consider whistleblower protection as an important factor in your small business's commitment to total quality management. Reward individuals who report problems with internal controls or procedures!

They just saved your small business time, money, and labor. The report might also have identified a problem that, ignored over time, could have resulted in a crisis.

Framework for Fraud

Fraud and fraudulent activities don't happen overnight. There are always supporting factors within a small business that facilitate opportunities for fraud. These include:

- *Incentive.* Individuals who engage in fraudulent activities want to steal, and either don't believe they will be caught or believe that there will be few, if any, consequences for their behavior. Lack of controls provides the incentive.

- *Occasion for the fraud to take place.* When there are weak or nonexistent internal controls the opportunity presents itself to engage in fraudulent activities. Access to petty cash or other assets that are quickly converted to cash are common examples.

- *Sloppy or nonexistent internal controls.* A wrongdoer can easily cover his or her tracks when there are no protocols or no records are kept.

- *Access to electronic databases and online checking.* Often, in order to cover fraud, the perpetrator will have to alter electronic records. Thus, those individuals who have access to sensitive databases are in a position to set up sham accounts and issue checks to themselves.

- *A culture of denial.* In a business that either denies the possibility of anyone committing fraud, unethical or disgruntled employees may take that stance as an invitation to prove them wrong. Even more insidious is a business culture that transforms employees into martyrs—how many times have you heard people say, "We work so hard here for so little money."

- *A business owner and/or management team "asleep at the wheel."* Stories abound about small business victims of fraud whose owners and senior management swear they knew nothing about it nor suspected anything. That's one of the most important reasons why you, a small business owner, must lead the way—talk about fraud and institute and enforce antifraud measures.

Again, Sarbanes-Oxley requirements provide individuals the opportunity and means to report waste, fraud, or abuse without fear of retaliation. Document preservation (discussed in detail in the next section) will facilitate more efficient record-keeping and provide auditors (external and internal) with better data for their review. The overall strengthening of the internal controls that comes with the implementation of best practices will further reduce the opportunities for fraud, and will introduce a change in the business culture.

Talking Points in the Discussion about Fraud

As stated repeatedly, you, the business owner, have to lead the way in talking about fraud, and be the visible source of policymaking in this area. When you talk about fraud, be candid about the factors that support fraudulent activities, and why the implementation of SOX requirements and best practices will help your business reduce the potential for such misdeeds within its operations. It is equally important to emphasize that you and the rest of management are committed to whistleblower protection; specifically, that any type of retaliation is to be reported directly to a designated management member or you, the business owner.

Don't be sidetracked in this important effort by a long-time manager or employee whose "feelings might be hurt" if you institute changes to protocols and expectations. The well-being of your small business comes first. These individuals will just have to "get over it" if they want to remain on the staff of your small business.

With those guidelines in mind, note that your small business's policies and procedures on whistleblower protection should contain the following features:

- *Confidential means for reporting suspected waste, fraud, and abuse.* Employees need to know precisely how to go about filing reports and what types of evidence they will need to provide to substantiate their claims.

- *Process to thoroughly investigate reports.* Employees should also understand how investigations will be conducted, specifically, what will be expected of them in terms of providing a further statement or answering questions.

- *Process for disseminating the findings from the investigation.* Whistleblowers should also be told how the findings of the report will be disseminated.

- *Protection against retribution for filing reports.* This is the most important part of the whistleblower protection policy. Protection mechanisms must be in place to protect all employees filing complaints from being subjected to termination, harassment, or failure to be promoted. And all employees should be informed what their rights are under the policy. It's important also that employees know that even if the investigation findings do not support the essence of their complaint, they will be protected against any repercussions.

In addition to your discussion with your employees regarding the company's whistleblower protection policy, it's a good idea to have one of your professional advisors talk to employees about fraud. The perspective of a financial professional, such as your banker or auditor, will serve to reinforce your message that you are committed to addressing fraudulent activities, which can inflict tremendous damage to any business. Your financial professional can also offer guidelines to your employees about basic fraud protection and their role in deterring fraud. Communication is key to ensuring that all employees understand why reporting waste, fraud, and abuse is company policy, what their rights are, and how investigations are conducted and findings presented.

Implementation of the Whistleblower Protection Policy

Give every employee a copy of your company's whistleblower policy and make it readily available for review in hard copy and online. And remember to cover the policy in any orientation or training programs the business provides to its employees. Again, the policy should clearly describe why whistleblower protection is necessary and how to file a

EXHIBIT 3.2   SAMPLE WHISTLEBLOWER POLICY

Huxley's Pet Shop Whistleblower Protection Policy

Talking Points

Why the Policy Is Being Implemented

The whistleblower protection policy is being implemented at Huxley's Pet Shop to comply with the Public Company Accounting Reform and Investor Protection Act of 2002 (Sarbanes-Oxley). This provision in the legislation applies to all companies, not just publicly traded ones.

The Company's Commitment to Protect Employees against Retribution for Filing a Report of Waste, Fraud, or Abuse

At Huxley's Pet Shop, any employee who reports waste, fraud, or abuse will not be fired or otherwise retaliated against for making the report. The report will be investigated and even if the situation is not determined to be waste, fraud, or abuse, the individual making the report will not be subject to retaliation. There will be no punishment such as firing, demotion, suspension, harassment, failure to consider the employee for promotion, or any other kind of discrimination for reporting problems.

How to Make a Report

There are several ways employees can make a report of suspected waste, fraud, or abuse:

- Call the Fictitious Anonymous Hotline.
- Send an email to fraudreports@huxleyspetshop.com.
- Submit a report in writing to the manager in charge of receiving these reports.

How the Report Will Be Investigated and Findings Disseminated

Here is what we will do to investigate the report:

[Huxley's Pet Shop would list the steps it would take to investigate the allegation.] Here is how we will follow up to report on our findings:

- Provide the person filing the report with a summary of our findings.
- Take steps to deal with the issue addressed, including making operational or personnel changes.
- If warranted, contact law enforcement to deal with any criminal activities.

Investigating the Report

[Huxley's would list the steps it would take to:]

- Investigate the allegation.
- Disseminate the report on our findings, including providing the person filing a report with a summary of the findings.
- Take steps to deal with the issue addressed, including making operational or personnel changes.
- If warranted, contact law enforcement to deal with any criminal activities.

Note: Be sure to have your legal counsel review and approve the language of your Whistleblower Protection Policy.

report, and state in no uncertain terms the company's commitment to protecting whistleblowers from retaliation.

It's also vitally important that your company's legal counsel review the wording of the whistleblower protection policy before it is released. Counsel should also be available to provide advice whenever whistleblower reports are filed.

Exhibit 3.2 contains a sample of the talking points an effective whistleblower protection policy should have.

DOCUMENT MANAGEMENT AND PRESERVATION POLICY

Of the many factors that contributed to the Enron and Arthur Andersen scandals, described in Chapter 1, the blatant attempts to destroy evidence by shredding documents stand out as particularly egregious. In fact, it was these deliberate acts that served as the catalyst for the SOX prohibition against destroying documents during an investigation or during legal proceedings. This prohibition came along with a more general document preservation policy that applies to all companies, public and private.

Some key areas for consideration in crafting and implementing a document preservation policy include:

- Which documents and records should be preserved and why?
- Are the documents in paper form only or are electronic files included? Which ones?
- How should email and instant messaging be handled?
- What are the expectations about the way documents are stored or archived and the ability to retrieve documents?
- How long is it necessary to keep these documents?
- Is there a protocol for disposing of documents once their storage time has elapsed?
- When should you not destroy materials?
- How can you make sure that everyone in your small business understands and adheres to these requirements?

EXHIBIT 3.3	SAMPLE MINIMUM STORAGE REQUIREMENTS

Document	Storage
Accounts receivable and payable ledgers	7 years
Articles of incorporation, charter, bylaws, minutes	Permanently
Bank reconciliation	3 years
Bank statements, electronic fund transfers, and canceled checks	3 years
Contracts, mortgages, notes, and leases (expired)	7 years
Deeds, mortgages, and bills of sale	Permanently
Payroll records	7 years
Contracts still in effect	Permanently
Correspondence—legal	Permanently
Correspondence—vendors	2 years
Tax returns and worksheets	Permanently
Grants (funded)	7 years after closure

Source: National Association of Veterans Research and Education Foundations

Exhibit 3.3 itemizes sample minimum storage requirements. The written document preservation policy should:

- *Describe the document retention policy.* Begin by stating that document retention is required by law. It is important that employees understand that document preservation is a component of SOX that applies to all companies, not just publicly traded firms.

- *Identify new procedures.* Specifically, these are the procedures that have emerged from the best practices regarding document preservation. Employees need to understand how to be in compliance, and what specific actions are required. They also need to understand the quality issues raised by these new behaviors and the scope of their accountability.

- *Identify and explain the obligations of individual employees.* This is essential to ensure that your small business is in compliance. Requirements for employees should be presented in writing, as part of their annual performance objectives or as part of their quarterly or semiannual performance review. And, because document preservation is probably a new requirement in your company, it is particularly important to make the guidelines for implementation user-friendly—that is, easy to understand and easy to put into practice.

- *Describe expectations, procedures, and consequences.* Detail what is expected of your employees in terms of new behaviors; clearly explain new procedures, along with the consequences for failing to adhere to them. It is particularly important that management be prepared to carry out these consequences, and swiftly, to send a strong message throughout the company that breaches will not be tolerated.

Management needs to coordinate the activities inherent to the implementation of a document preservation policy. Fortunately, since most of today's documents are stored in electronic format, implementing the specifics of the plan can be streamlined. The system you design for document storage, archiving, and retrieval must be logical and user-friendly. It is essential that everyone in the company—beginning with you, the owner, to senior managers and to the newest clerical employee—understands what is expected of them. If employees can't make heads or tails of what the policy is about, what's expected of them, and why they are being asked to do this, then the probability of compliance is low.

Your Small Business Technology Policy: Companion Piece to Document Preservation

An important companion piece to the document preservation policy is a technology policy. Because the misuse of the technologies in a small business can cause serious liability for the company, management has to design a policy to address the use of all types of technology that are used within the company—including email, Internet access, voicemail, cell phones, laptops, PDAs, faxes, and all other equipment owned by the small business. Your company's technology policy should include, at a minimum, these talking points:

- *Clearly state that all aspects of your company's technology belongs to it.* There are *no* expectations of personal privacy when using the technology that is the property of the small business.

- *Identify all items of the small business's technology.* This means both hardware and software, including laptop and desktop computers; hand-held devices such as PDAs and BlackBerry devices and cell phones; and Internet access, email, and all software programs purchased through the small business. Be aware that when electronic devices such as laptops or PDAs are "recycled" to another employee member, the hard drive of the device may still contain data, documents, or transactions from the previous user. Therefore, before passing the device on to a new user, it is important to institute a procedure to erase the hard drive once all of the documents have been extracted and stored according to your small business's document retention policy.

- *Develop a policy to address the storage of sensitive information, as well as its transportation out of your company facilities.* Reports abound describing incidents of laptops being stolen that contained sensitive data. The same thing could happen to your small business if you store sensitive information about customers, clients, or employees on laptops that leave your premises.

Once you have defined your company's technology policy, be sure to have your legal counsel review and approve the language of it. Then, brief all employees on it; give them a copy of the policy; and along with it, distribute a letter, for their signature, wherein they state that they have been briefed on the technology policy and pledge to comply with it.

Documents on Your Small Business Web Site

Your small business's Web site is the electronic "face" of your company. The way it is designed, its features (which, ideally, make it user-friendly), and its content all say important things about your company. Some small businesses utilize their Web sites to collect donations for charities they sponsor, to sell merchandise, or even to respond to a global disaster. In light of these myriad uses, your company's document preservation policy should also address those "documents" that are pages on the Web site, such as:

- Your small business's annual financials, if they are part of an annual report

- Documents that demonstrate SOX compliance and best practices, such as your whistleblower protection and document preservation policies

- Reports, information about management members, programs, annual reports, and financial reports

And because security is now one of the major challenges facing the owners of company Web sites—whether small business or private sector—all Web sites need to have firewalls and encryption software to protect customer information and to ensure that transactions online with customers are secure. When customers put a credit card number on your Web site, for example, they and you need to feel confident that this sensitive information is properly encrypted and transported to the correct location and is not accessible to prying "eyes." As a further protection to your customers, you should also consider including user safety recommendations on your Web site regarding online transactions. For example, recommend that customers use a credit card, rather than a debit card, and that they check their credit card statements to ensure that all the transactions are accurate. And, if possible, include a link to your local Better Business Bureau, Chamber of Commerce, or small business clearinghouse, where customers can go to verify that your small business is a member in good standing.

NEXT STEPS

Whistleblower protection and document preservation are the two SOX requirements for private companies. To summarize the important points of these requirements:

- Whistleblower protection is one of the best defenses against waste, fraud, and abuse. But because of the intense media attention on certain well-known cases of whistleblower retaliation, it is vital that your company's policy include provisions to ensure that your employees are given a safe and confidential method for making reports.

• The prohibition against destroying documents requires companies to track important documents—even those it might find troublesome in the future. Managers and employees are required to ensure that electronic and paper copies are appropriately stored and easily retrievable.

In Chapter 6 we will examine the strategies for implementing these requirements.

CHAPTER 4

Best Practices from Sarbanes-Oxley: The New Gold Standard for Management

> *Instead of viewing SOX as merely one of the many compliance hurdles they face today, small business managers/owners need to think of it as an opportunity to improve corporate governance, policies and procedures and to reduce corporate costs. From an auditor's viewpoint, I believe a tremendous opportunity has emerged to incorporate the results of SOX testing (identified deficiencies and best practices) into future assessments, scoping of internal audits, reengineering, and other processes.*
>
> MATTHEW A. COZAD (2005)

This chapter will explore the ways SOX requirements for publicly traded companies have emerged as best practices for small businesses. Emphasis will be on the return on investment (ROI) for efforts made to incorporate these best practices. By implementing these practices, small businesses can develop a more solid infrastructure, along with efficiencies of scale, which will serve to facilitate greater confidence in their dealings with current and potential customers, and ease the procurement of insurance and other financial products.

THE BEST PRACTICES

The best practices that will be covered in this chapter include:

- *Upgrading the current quality of audits by means of auditor independence and an audit committee.* The individual who conducts the company's audit should not be involved in any other services to the company, such as tax preparation or consulting. If the company has a board, the executive committee needs to appoint an audit committee, whose role also includes the upgrade of the financial literacy of management and corporate board.

- *Ensuring accuracy of certified financial statements.* The management in any small business is ultimately accountable for the accuracy and integrity of the company's financial statements, as well as its tax return. The company needs to ensure that the CEO or CFO can validate the accuracy of the business's financial statements

- *Instituting a higher level of management accountability.* This includes upgrading policies and procedures for management accountability, adding new management orientation, and specifying performance expectations.

- *Establishing a conflict of interest policy.* This policy will apply to the company board (if there is one), managers, and employees to facilitate a sharper focus on decision-making processes, for the good of the business.

- *Developing a code of ethics.* This code must apply to the company board (if there is one), managers, and employees. It should preclude any loans to directors, officers, managers, or employees of the business. The code of ethics should also address gifts or other potential "kickbacks" from vendors.

- *Implementing internal controls.* In particular, these relate to financial operations and to compliance with all laws and regulations at the federal, state, and local levels.

- *Segregating duties* to ensure that employees have distinct duties related to finance or handling of other assets to reduce the potential for manipulation or fraud.

- *Recognizing the role of technology in the company's internal controls.* Your company's technology system serves as the framework for ensuring that internal controls are in compliance. Your auditor can assist in identifying any flaws in your company's processes or internal controls. Once these have been identified, it is imperative to remedy them at once, even if it means acquiring additional resources (Van Orden, 2004).

- *Ensuring transparency at all levels of management and in all transactions.* This includes all travel claims and reimbursements. Issues surrounding transparency are often the primary catalysts in initiating an investigation that uncovers widespread fraud within the company.

- *Assuring consistent adherence to and enforcement of new policies and procedures.* Management will not be successful in its endeavors to bring the business into SOX compliance unless the new policies and procedures are stringently enforced.

Instituting Best Practices into Small Business Operations

Upgrading the Current Quality of Audits by Means of Auditor Independence and an Audit Committee

The independence of auditors is a key best practice. As just noted, the person who conducts your company's audit should not be involved in any other services to the company such as tax preparation or consulting. In the past, it was a common practice for an accounting firm to offer an array of services, including auditing, to small businesses. This is no longer the case. If your company auditor is currently providing any services other than auditing to the company, you should consider retaining another firm to conduct the audit (Beasley, et al., 2001; Anthony, 2005).

Do not overlook the auditor's role in helping your small business implement SOX requirements and best practices. Without the auditor's input in terms of current gaps and deficiencies, your efforts to implement SOX requirements and best practices could be ineffective. Look to your auditor as a source of valuable information on how you can leverage SOX compliance and best practices to strengthen your company's overall health (Jefferson Wells, 2005).

The audit committee's role is to oversee the annual audit or financial review (for small businesses) and to upgrade the financial "literacy" of management and members of the corporate board (if one exists). The audit committee is the link between management, the board, and its auditor or financial reviewer. It is an important element in ensuring that management understands the results of the annual audit or financial review for *really* small businesses.

Ensuring Accuracy of Certified Financial Statements

The business owner(s)/managers are ultimately accountable for the accuracy and integrity of the company's financial statements, as well as its tax return. Therefore, the CEO or CFO must be able to validate the accuracy of the business's financial statements. The role of IT is particularly significant, in that management should recognize that there may be a gap between finance controls and IT controls, and this gap will need to be bridged by making necessary modifications to the controls (Jefferson Wells, 2005).

Instituting a Higher Level of Management Accountability

The new paradigm of higher management accountability includes upgraded policies and procedures for management accountability, new management orientation, and performance expectations.

Establishing a Conflict of Interest Policy

Many of the corporate crisis scenarios in the recent past resulted from blatant self-dealing. This is one of the most troublesome aspects of corporate fraud. To guard against this, businesses of any size need to establish effective conflict of interest policies that identify real or potential conflicts of interest; and management and key employees should be required to sign a statement to the effect that they have no conflicts of interest. The enforcement of a conflict of interest policy facilitates greater focus on decision making for the good of the business.

Developing a Code of Ethics

All businesses need a code of ethics to guide the conduct of management and employees. This code should explicitly preclude any loans to directors, officers, managers, or employees of the business. The code of ethics should also address gifts or other potential "kickbacks" from vendors. "These codes typically cover conflicts of interest, confidentiality, fair dealing, protection of company assets, compliance with laws, and encouraging the reporting of illegal or unethical behavior . . . and may provide some legal protection if a company is sued for misconduct and the company can demonstrate that it has a code of ethics and diligently attempted to follow it" (Lieberman, 2004).

Implementing Internal Controls

Internal controls, especially relating to financial operations and compliance with all laws and regulations at the federal, state, and local levels, are at the heart of SOX requirements. The internal audit is an important mechanism to ensure that internal controls are in place and followed. Internal controls can also be reviewed and certified as effective by the company's auditor (Lieberman, 2004).

Segregating Duties

This best practice requires the company to clearly define employees' roles and responsibilities and to segregate those duties related to finance or handling of other assets. "The basic idea underlying segregation of duties is that no employee or group should be in a position both to perpetrate and to conceal errors or fraud in the normal course of their duties. . . . The use of checklists to define an employee's job responsibility and accountability is a good method to ensure that duties are genuinely separate. Management should also consider updating policies and procedures and evaluating current policies in light of SOX requirements and best practices" (Cozad, 2005).

Recognizing the Role of Technology in SOX Compliance and Best Practices

"Information technology is the backbone of the financial processes the law requires. . . . Work with your company's auditor to find process and internal control flaws in information technology systems" (Van Orden, 2004). SOX best practices recognize the pivotal role that IT plays in company operations, not only in organizing data for operational application, but in how financial data is recorded and analyzed. In fact, IT plays a significant role in virtually every aspect of SOX requirements and best practices. Too often, small businesses overlook this aspect of management because their companies may only use standard software programs.

Ensuring Transparency at All Levels of Management

It is imperative that management (1) insist on written procedures for filing travel and reimbursement claims and (2) ensure that these procedures be enforced—even by means of unannounced audits. Methods of enforcement include:

- Review current compliance activities and identify ways to reduce the number of key controls.
- Increase the use of controls self-assessments.
- Improve the overall control environment to better match compliance efforts to risk. Implement an ongoing fraud and risk management process to reduce losses.
- Improve the finance organization's capabilities.

By focusing on the value provided by the finance function, organizations will naturally improve governance and controls (Jefferson Wells, 2005).

Assuring Consistent Adherence and Enforcement of the Policies and Procedures

Management will not be successful in its endeavors to bring the business into SOX compliance or be able to implement best practices unless the new policies and procedures are enforced. Rewards and consequences that correspond with desired behavior will have to be implemented to achieve these goals.

THE ROI OF BEST PRACTICES

The tangible benefits associated with the implementation of SOX best practices are numerous:

- *Governance.* If your small business has a board, compliance with Sarbanes-Oxley requirements and adaptation of best practices will make your board a more effective entity. Its members will understand and thus be able to adhere to their fiduciary obligations, and recognize their responsibility in governing the company. Additionally, good governance is an important factor in making the firm an attractive candidate for acquisition.

- *Accountability.* SOX best practices introduce higher levels of management and employee accountability, including more reliable financial reports and other evidence of solid internal controls. Effective internal controls also serve as a deterrent to fraudulent activities and shrinkage of inventory.

- *Operations.* Effective protocols serve to ensure that the company remains in compliance with SOX and the company's "industry standards," and addresses future standards, particularly if the company is considering launching an IPO.

- *Marketing.* When it is known that your company adheres to the SOX gold standard in its operating practices, it is better positioned competitively.

- *Strategic positioning.* Complying with SOX and implementing its best practices gives your company greater credibility and ability to attract necessary resources, be these in the form of high-quality *independent* board members, sources of capital, business partners, or other fund sources.

- *Reduced litigation exposure.* The directors of private and public companies are legally obligated to satisfy their fiduciary duties. To the extent that governance practices of public companies have established higher standards of director conduct, courts are likely to look to those standards to determine whether directors have exercised the requisite degree of care and loyalty (Lieberman, 2004).

- *Positioning to launch an IPO.* Complying with SOX will require substantial planning and resources, so a company contemplating an IPO should prepare to comply with SOX well in advance (Lieberman, 2004).

The best practices that have emerged from SOX legislation offer small businesses the means to strengthen their internal controls. Today's business environment has raised the expectations for all companies, not just publicly traded ones. The gold standard in management today is SOX compliance, regardless of the size of your company. If you want your firm to remain competitive, the implementation of these best practices is a must.

NEXT STEPS

In Chapters 3 and 4 we examined the SOX requirements and best practices. Chapter 5 introduces a Blueprint that will facilitate implementation of SOX compliance and best practices in a comprehensive approach.

Establishing a Blueprint for Success

Blueprint: a detailed plan or program of action
—MERRIAM-WEBSTER ONLINE DICTIONARY

BLUEPRINT FOR IMPLEMENTATION OF SOX REQUIREMENTS AND BEST PRACTICES

The concept of a blueprint represents a documented plan or design of action; it can also include subsidiary constructs and additional elements, which support the whole structure. Using this concept, this chapter will present a streamlined model for implementation of SOX requirements and best practices. And though the Blueprint introduced here takes its inspiration from the traditional COSO Internal Controls–Integrated Framework, it specifically considers the resource constraints faced by small businesses. It has been developed to facilitate the incorporation of SOX requirements and best practices with the realities of today's small business working environment as its foundation (e.g., smaller employee levels, marginal discretionary income, and extensive local regulatory requirements).

The Blueprint's primary function is to assist small businesses in taking the steps necessary to achieve compliance and adaptation of best practices. Following the traditional use of a blueprint, small businesses can use this one as a tool to visualize the future structure of their operations and to plan how these operations might be further supported by ongoing practices such as risk management and business continuity planning—that is, a continuum of planning.

IMPLEMENTING THE BLUEPRINT

If you were working with an architect on a remodeling project, the first step you would take would be to review the current structure—to determine what needs to be done and how to begin. Similarly, as you begin to contemplate implementation of SOX requirements and best practices in your small business, it is important to first gauge your company's current status. The point is to determine how to take those actions necessary to move your small business along on the success continuum. By knowing your company's current profile you can more easily comply with SOX requirements and introduce its best practices. This foreknowledge also will provide an important point of reference for subsequent improvements. Finally, understanding where your company is in terms of compliance will also help you identify those areas that should be given priority attention, and assist in establishing a sequence of activities to produce lasting results.

Following the Blueprint requires you to take these five steps (illustrated in Exhibit 5.1):

1. Examine your company's style and culture.
2. Identify what has the potential to damage your business operations or reputation.
3. Identify your standard operating procedures (SOPs) in terms of what you currently have and what you need.
4. Ensure everyone is on the same page.
5. Verify that the SOPs are working.

The Blueprint is constructed using these five steps:

1. Examine your company's style and culture.
2. Identify what could damage your business's operations or reputation.
3. Identify your standard operating procedures (SOPs) in terms of what you currently have and what you need.
4. Ensure everyone is on the same page.
5. Verify that the SOPs are working.

```
┌─────────┐     ┌─────────┐     ┌─────────┐     ┌─────────┐
│  Your   │     │  What   │     │ SOPs—   │     │Ensuring │
│company's│ ──▶ │ could   │ ──▶ │what you │ ──▶ │everyone │
│style and│     │ damage  │     │have and │     │is on the│
│ culture │     │  your   │     │what you │     │same page│
│         │     │business?│     │  need   │     │         │
└─────────┘     └─────────┘     └─────────┘     └─────────┘
                                                      │
                                                      ▼
                               ┌──────────────────────────┐
                               │  Ensuring the SOPs are    │
                               │        working!           │
                               └──────────────────────────┘
```

EXHIBIT 5.1   Blueprint

Step 1: Examine Your Company's Style and Culture

Your company's style and culture comprises both the intangible and perceptible environment of the organization. The culture encompasses how you, the owner, and the company managers articulate the organizational values and principles, which includes how you and management set the current parameters for rewards and punishment. In many small business environments, owners and/or managers will take the first step of articulating the company's values and guidelines for specific types of behavior, but fail to follow through by rewarding individuals who adopt the behavior (or, conversely, punishing those who don't). When you fail to reward desired behavior, it can lead to employee discouragement and, ultimately, to the very behavior you were trying to prevent! Likewise, by failing to mete out timely and specific penalties for undesirable behavior, you will be reinforcing it. If you as an owner or manager don't understand why employees continue to behave in a manner you disapprove of, ask yourself when was the last time they witnessed someone in the company being held accountable for their actions. Empty threats are just that: empty. Both managers and employees need to understand that stated consequences will immediate and enforced unequivocally.

The point of this step is to candidly assess how well your managers and employees follow directives and adapt to new practices. If the answer is not very well, then you will have to dramatically change your system of rewards and consequences, and be prepared to implement them quickly and in no uncertain terms. It is a new day in your company, and you will need to send out this message, loud and clear: *Compliance with new policies and procedures is an absolute condition of continued employment.*

If your company has a board, taking this step will also help you to assess its productivity and effectiveness. As you consider the board's composition and the skill sets of its members, attention to legal principles of governance (care, loyalty, and obedience) and commitment to fiduciary obligations are key. Subsequently, you will be able to determine if you need any new and independent board members (independence is particularly significant if the composition of the board is primarily family members).

Step 2: Identify What Has Potential to Damage Your Business Operations or Reputation

Unfortunately, there are innumerable ways your small business could be damaged and/or the reputation of your company tarnished. The point of this step is to consider what the larger issues are in terms of managing risk within your company; it is *not* to become bogged down in drawing unending what-if scenarios. For the purposes of this discussion of the Blueprint, you will want to consider the risks of failure to adopt SOX requirements and best practices.

An effective way to organize the identification of risk areas is to start by identifying and assessing these risk areas: the company's governance and management, HR, operations, and public image of the organization.

Governance and Management

In this area of your business you will address those risks associated with executive activity, including board membership, deliberations, and governance issues. For example, risk may center around a lack of routinely scheduled board meetings, if the company has a board. Decision-making models that are autocratic or lack reasonable due diligence can pose problems. Conflict of interest issues, too, are a significant source of problems in this area, particularly if members of management team are silent partners in firms doing business with your company. Appropriate insurance coverage, such as directors and officers (D&O) insurance, should be considered, as well as insurance to cover employment practices liability.

Some common problems associated with governance and management include:

- The company does not have a conflict of interest policy or a code of ethics. Managers are not held accountable for use of company credit cards or expense accounts.
- The board consists primarily of family members.
- The board does not have term limits, and board members have been in place for over five years.

- Board members don't attend meetings.
- Board meetings don't follow agendas or keep minutes.
- The board does not have D&O insurance.

Human Resources

This human resources component of the company structure dictates how it manages its human "capital," its employees. In assessing risks, you'll want to consider the company's practices in recruitment, hiring, retention, supervision, and termination. Other risk areas include lack of a whistleblower protection policy; Americans with Disabilities Act (ADA) compliance; supervisory practices; compensation issues; and grievance procedures for issues other than waste, fraud, and abuse.

Some common causes of HR-related problems include:

- Employees do not have job descriptions, and are not evaluated on a regular basis.
- There are no written policies regarding sick leave, vacation, or other paid or unpaid time off.
- There are no written policies addressing inappropriate behavior such as sexual harassment or drug/alcohol abuse.
- Off-site managers (located in branch offices or stores) do not understand their obligations to the company.
- There is no employee manual.

Operations

For the purposes of implementing the Blueprint, in this discussion "operations" is used to describe all of the major divisions that carry out the work of the company. These typically include:

- Finance
- Administration
- Sales and marketing
- Information technology (IT)

- Inventory and warehouse
- Transportation
- Customer relationship and service
- Legal compliance
  - Federal regulations (including Sarbanes-Oxley)
  - State regulations
  - Local ordinances

Common problems associated with operations include:

- Lack of internal controls for financial operations
  - Travel claims are not processed in a consistent manner.
  - Reimbursements are subject to arbitrary measures. For example, senior management is not required to provide the same level of documentation for a reimbursement claim as are members of the rank and file.
  - Monthly financial statements are not prepared in a manner consistent with GAAP.
- Documents are not stored or archived in a user-friendly fashion, nor are they easily retrievable.
- Reports either are submitted late or are prepared at the last minute.
- Procedures for oversight of inventory and warehousing need to be strengthened.
- No inventory exists for IT supplies and electronics. There are no procedures for tracking and retrieving electronic devices before employees leave the company.

Public Relations

Never forget: Your company operates within a society that emphasizes the rule of law and expects the private sector to behave in an ethical manner. By safeguarding your company's good image and reputation, you will keep it off the radar screens of consumer watchdog groups, public sector regulatory agencies, and law enforcement. In short, it is essential that your company maintain good relationships with its customers and the community at large by putting effective public and media relations systems in place.

Common problems to avoid in this risk assessment area include:

- The company lacks an effective method for handling complaints from customers and neighbors.
- The company does not have a crisis management plan.
- The company does not cultivate media relations.

As you consider these general risk areas within your small business, prioritize those that deal with SOX requirements and best practices and develop strategies for dealing with each of them. It is important to reiterate that the routine practice of identifying risks and crafting strategies for dealing with them is an essential component to an effective risk management plan. You'll gain additional value from risk management practices by having business continuity plan, which will facilitate your company's swift recovery from any kind of business interruption. (More on risk management and business continuity plans later in the chapter.)

Step 3: Identify Your Company's Standard Operating Procedures

In this step you will identify your company's current internal controls and determine whether they have been integrated effectively within the company's technology infrastructure. Additionally, you will determine which SOX requirements and best practices will have to be implemented to achieve total compliance. You can use the condensed risk assessment defined in step 2 to illustrate gaps in documenting processes and/or ensuring standardized policies and procedures. It is important, however, to caution against getting bogged down in this process. For now, concentrate on those SOPs that relate to SOX requirements and best practices. Keep in mind that you will need to review and upgrade your company's SOPs on a regular basis.

Step 4: Ensure That Everyone Is on the Same Page

As you put new policies, procedures, and practices into place in your small business, good communication becomes essential. Everyone in the organization has to know what he or she is expected to do to support internal control activities and objectives. Likewise, everyone in the organization, from board members to rank-and-file employees must understand overall performance objectives.

Therefore, you will need to establish a communication framework to ensure that internal control activities are standardized. Communication and training can be done via the company's intranet, in specific training or "in-service" sessions, or on a departmental basis. The key element is to find a way to keep everyone in the company informed on a timely basis as to changing policies, procedures, and expectations.

Step 5: Verify That the SOPs Are Working

To complete this step, your company's internal control activities will have to be continuously monitored to ensure they remain relevant to the current business environment and can be readily adapted to meet changing benchmarks of quality. Unannounced internal audits can be particularly effective in ascertaining that policies, procedures, and internal controls—particularly those related to SOX compliance—are enforced. The emphasis should be on rewarding compliance, but the underlying message should be that penalties for noncompliance will be swiftly applied.

Step Summary

Once you have completed this five-step process, your company will have a Blueprint that illustrates your current status as well as the actions you need to take to come into SOX compliance and best practices. The Blueprint can also be used to jump-start effective risk management and business continuity plans, which are discussed next.

USING THE BLUEPRINT AS THE FOUNDATION FOR EFFECTIVE RISK MANAGEMENT AND BUSINESS CONTINUITY PLANS

Implementing SOX requirements and best practices offers opportunities to add value in other areas of business planning. Specifically, using the Blueprint to organize your SOX compliance and best practices paves the way for your company to develop efficient risk management and business continuity plans. (Note that SOX implementation, risk management, and business continuity planning all have overlapping activities and values, and Chapter 8 will present methods for streamlining implementation of these plans.)

Defining Risk Management and Business Continuity Planning

Risk Management

Risk management is the means by which companies can identify, assess, and control risks that may be present within their infrastructure or operations. It is an ongoing process that works only when it is thoroughly integrated into the company's operations. SOX best practices have a "value-added" component, in that they can be used to identify the means of mitigating risks associated with fiduciary obligations, legal compliance, board governance, and other areas. The areas to examine in an effective risk management plan are often the same as those addressed in SOX requirements and best practices.

When the topic of business continuity or contingency planning is raised, many people think first of natural disasters, such as hurricanes, floods, earthquakes, and the like. The reality is more likely that the operations at your company will be interrupted by a key person leaving, becoming ill, or dying. Or, a fire in an adjoining office might cause your building to be "red tagged," declared off limits by local authorities; the smoke and water damage from that fire could destroy your offices or necessitate extensive repairs. Even a sudden loss of electricity or the introduction of a computer virus transmitted through the Internet could destroy your company's databases and electronic files.

Business Continuity Planning

Business continuity planning (BCP) is the process of (1) designing strategies for preventing unnecessarily long-term interruption to company operations, by establishing back-up systems to preserve the company's assets, files, records, and other essential components; and (2) developing procedures for resuming, as soon as possible, essential business operations following a business interruption, should one occur. The implementation of SOX requirements and best practices and any state laws that would apply to your company can be easily leveraged to facilitate the design of an effective BCP. By virtue of taking these steps, your company can easily incorporate them into the elements of a BCP.

Once you have an effective plan, it's important to share the plan, and your best practices, with your insurance professional, because the insurance industry today is calling for proof of contingency planning from its commercial clients. Having a BCP demonstrates that the company intends to remain a viable entity, ready to serve, regardless of what happens. The plan also serves to position your company more favorably when it comes time to negotiate rates for business interruption and extra expense coverage. Your insurance professional can advise you on these matters.

The rollout of your company's BCP is vital to maintaining the confidence and trust of customers, suppliers, employees, and other stakeholders. The provisions of the plan will help your company remain in compliance with federal and state regulations regarding document preservation, submission of required materials such as an IRS Form, tax return, and other requirements.

Developing a BCP that is ready for immediate implementation is also a clear demonstration of your company's commitment to accountability, as it will also enable you to provide support to clients and employees who may be experiencing the impact of the business interruption, whatever form it takes.

How These Plans Add Value to SOX Compliance and Best Practices

SOX requirements and best practices are benchmarks for a rational and productive response to crisis events, whether in the form of a natural disaster, fire, loss of a key employee, an accident involving an employee, or other crisis scenario. With these plans in place, investigations into such events will be more productive and accurate because you and your employees will be able to easily retrieve relevant documents and files, thanks to your "no-destroy" policy. The plans will also safeguard the protocols that ensure the company remains in compliance with SOX and industry standards and addresses future standards.

NEXT STEPS

The activities associated with the implementation of SOX requirements and best practices can be organized via the Blueprint model defined here. It is designed to streamline the process and to ensure that your company policies and procedures are consistent with its culture and can be easily understood by employees. The Blueprint also identifies those areas of your company's culture or practices that need to be modified to ensure employees adhere to SOX requirements and best practices. Chapters 6 and 7 explain further how to utilize the Blueprint to introduce strategies to implement SOX requirements and best practices.

CHAPTER 6

The Blueprint and SOX Requirements

Susan is the owner of a small business that provides engineering services. She is a supplier for the XYZ Company, which has a multimillion dollar contract with the U.S. Department of Transportation (DOT). Susan faces a dilemma: The XYZ Company has come under investigation for fraudulent billing practices with the DOT, and Susan's records contain files that would be helpful to the government's case. But XYZ Company is one of her biggest clients, and she knows that even if XYZ is exonerated, her cooperation with the federal investigators will undoubtedly cause irreparable damage to her relationship with the company. Hence, her own company stands to lose millions of dollars in sales. She's looking at the firm's new super-turbo shredder as a way out of this mess.

Don't do it, Susan, or you might find yourself sleeping in the Martha Stewart suite at Camp Cupcake. ■

Intentional destruction of documents, even if your company has nothing to do with the fraud, can subject you to steep fines and up to 20 years in prison (Bahls and Bahls, 2003). The scope of this provision of Sarbanes-Oxley legislation applies to *every* company, private as well as public. Thus, in Susan's case, she has to ensure that any documents relevant to

XYZ Company are *not* destroyed; she also needs to contact her legal counsel to advise him or her of the situation, and to follow the advice she is given.

Remember, the SOX document preservation policy includes an important component that prohibits the destruction of documents during an investigation or legal action. This isn't limited to an investigation of your own company; it also includes any documents that could become evidence in the investigation or legal proceedings (Bahls and Bahls, 2003).

The essence of a company's culture may have to be restructured in order to introduce real and lasting change to meet the Sarbanes-Oxley requirements, and the primary change agents will have to be members of senior management. They will be responsible for beginning the process and implementing strategies along the way to institute a SOX-compliant perspective on the way their company does business and evaluates at its programs, its clients, its customers, its employees, even its future.

To ensure that you and your company's management is prepared for this undertaking, this chapter examines in greater depth how the Blueprint introduced in Chapter 5 can be utilized to organize the activities that your business must complete to come into compliance with the two Sarbanes-Oxley requirements—whistleblower protection and document preservation.

WHISTLEBLOWER PROTECTION

In Chapter 3 we examined the whistleblower protection requirements. Recall that this provision requires all businesses, including small companies, to establish a means to collect, retain, and resolve claims regarding accounting, internal accounting controls, and auditing matters. The system must allow such concerns to be submitted anonymously. This SOX requirement provides significant protections to whistleblowers, and severe penalties to those who fail to adhere to them.

To review, a whistleblower protection policy should contain at least the following features:

- Confidential avenue for reporting suspected waste, fraud, and abuse
- Process for thoroughly investigating any reports
- Process for disseminating the findings from the investigation
- Safeguards to ensure that whistleblowers will not be subjected to termination, firing, or harassment, or miss out on promotion— even if investigation findings do not support the nature of the complaint

Once your company's whistleblower policy is finalized, the last step is to disseminate a copy of it to all employees and to post in clear view on the company premises. Furthermore, the policy should be covered in any orientation or training programs the business offers for its employees.

Introducing Change

There are a number of tools senior management can use to focus attention and reinforce the changes once they are made (Exhibit 6.1 contains a checklist). The most important change element, necessary if SOX requirements are to "take," is the company's culture. As discussed previously, culture is reflected in the company's values and belief system, the way experiences (both positive and negative) are translated into lessons learned, and the ways new methods of operation are introduced.

Senior management can best introduce the changes that they expect to see, as well as the consequences for failure to adhere to the changes, by:

- *Clarifying measures of success.* Senior management controls the metrics used to measure quality in the company, so they will have to specify the new quality standards, including how these standards will be measured. As a result, both management and employees will need to adopt a new understanding of quality within the company.

EXHIBIT 6.1   **SENIOR MANAGEMENT COORDINATION OF SOX COMPLIANCE AND BEST PRACTICES CHECKLIST**

- If the company has a board, the senior management holds regular meetings with the board's executive committee.
- Senior management reviews the company's whistleblower protection policy to ensure that it is written in compliance with SOX requirements.
- Senior management reviews the mechanism for filing whistleblower complaints, to ensure the rights of whistleblowers are preserved.
- The company has a document preservation policy in place.
- The senior management has reviewed and approved a policy prohibiting the destruction of documents during an inquiry or legal action.
- Senior management has conducted (or is planning to conduct in the near future) a review of the company's internal controls.
- Senior management has developed a crisis communication plan for the company.
- Senior management has ensured that the procedures for all SOX requirements and best practices have been shared with all employees.
- Senior management has taken responsibility for conducting unannounced reviews of procedures and protocols, to ensure compliance.

- *Allocating financial and other resources to reinforce new values and expected change.* This may require making budgetary changes or reordering priorities, but the message needs to be that the budget will be developed in a way that directly supports implementation of SOX requirements and best practices. Managers who resist these changes should have their budgets reduced, or their divisions will need to be reorganized, and managers who support the implementation of best practices will be promoted. Resource reallocation may also take the form of changing the location of employee workstations or offices. Office "real estate" often comes laden with power implications, so relocating an individual's office can convey a powerful message.

- *Changing how both rewards and penalties are distributed.* It is important to reward desired behavior as well as to institute swift consequences for refusal to comply. It is equally important to present written performance expectations for all employees and to document actual performance.

- *Altering the way special recognition is conveyed.* Change the way employees are promoted, assigned to plum projects, or awarded special recognition to ensure that these rewards are clearly linked to the implementation of best practices.

The point of these actions is to enable employees to clearly see the connection between the desired behavior and positive reinforcement. Equally important, they also need to see that it is not only their behavior that is expected to change, but that of senior management as well.

Senior management's primary duties in following through on SOX compliance and best practices center on coordinating and providing oversight for the whistleblower protection policy. This includes designing a confidential reporting mechanism and investigation protocols; reviewing internal controls; and instituting a document preservation policy, with prohibitions against destroying documents during an investigation. The implementation of these two requirements establishes the framework for the next step, which is the enforcement of best practices.

Using the Blueprint to Create an Effective Whistleblower Protection Policy

As explained in Chapter 5, you can craft an effective whistleblower protection policy using the Blueprint. Remember, before finalizing the document, have your company's legal counsel review and approve the wording of the policy and any other documents that you produce.

In Chapter 5, five steps were itemized for using the Blueprint. Here, we'll delve into these further, by reformulating the steps as a series of questions.

Step 1: How Would You Define Your Company's Style and Culture?
The purpose of this question is to help you see how to leverage the best aspects of your company's culture to implement whistleblower protection and document preservation policies. Your company's style and culture are central to the introduction and effective adaptation of whistleblower protection. Frame what you will say to be consistent with the company's values and business style. Compliance comes more easily when the new practices are consistent with the work environment and company values. Employees need to understand that management is

committed to eliminating waste, fraud, and abuse in the company. They should also understand that early reporting of waste, fraud, and abuse saves millions of dollars and preserves the company's good name—thus, their job security.

Step 2: What Could Damage Your Company's Operations or Reputation?

As you prepare to implement a whistleblower protection policy, you will gain insight by considering how the absence of this policy might impact the company as a whole, as well as individual employees. Your findings will be important as you go about describing why management values those people who summon up the courage to file a report of suspected waste, fraud, or abuse.

Examples of damage the absence of a whistleblower protection policy could cause include:

- Wrongful termination litigation if an employee is fired for making a report

- Loss to the company of millions of dollars through fraud, embezzlement, and misappropriation of funds or assets

- Damage to the company's image and reputation following a scandal

Step 3: What Are Your Standard Operating Procedures (SOPs)?

Senior management should review the company's SOPs on whistleblower protection, to ensure that they are documented and enforced and contain the following features:

- *Confidential means for reporting suspected waste, fraud, and abuse.* Employees need to know how to go about filing a report and what types of evidence they will be expected to provide to substantiate their claims. Are there specific ways employees are expected to make the reports?

- *Process for thoroughly investigating reports.* Employees should also know how investigations will be conducted; specifically, what will be expected of them in terms of issuing a statement or answering questions.

- *Process for disseminating investigation findings.* The whistleblower should also know how the findings of the report will be disseminated.

- *Guarantees that no employee filing a complaint will be subjected to termination, firing, or harassment, or miss out on promotion.* This is the most important part of the policy, and it is vital that all employees know their rights under the company's whistleblower protection policy. They need assurances that even if the investigation findings do not support the nature of the complaint they will not face any repercussions.

Step 4: How Can You Ensure Everyone Is on the Same Page?

If your company is introducing whistleblower protection for the first time, it is important that all employees, from senior management to the newest hire, be thoroughly briefed on its contents. Be sure to: cover what their rights are if they file a report; identify the types of situations that warrant filing a report; and emphasize that without a mechanism for reporting waste, fraud, and abuse, the company could sustain devastating losses. During the briefing of whistleblower protection with your employees, be very clear to make these points:

- *A whistleblower is not a snitch.* Rather, a person who suspects waste, fraud, or abuse is *obligated* to report this to management. If the person's suspicions turn out to be correct he or she could be helping to preserve the company's good name and the jobs and benefits that all its employees enjoy.

- *A person who reports waste, fraud, or abuse has rights.* He or she cannot be terminated for making the report, nor be demoted, humiliated, or otherwise penalized for his or her actions. Management should reassure employees in this regard by instituting a hotline they can use to advise the owner(s) or CEO if they believe their rights are being infringed upon.

- *Even pilfering, shrinkage, and any other seemingly low-level theft needs to be reported.* When it is overlooked, the company suffers as does

EXHIBIT 6.2 **WHISTLEBLOWER PROTECTION POLICY CHECKLISTS**

Your company needs to have:
- A whistleblower protection policy
- A method for reporting waste, fraud, or abuse
- Procedures for conducting investigations
- Protocols for disseminating findings (in conjunction with your legal counsel)

Whistleblower Protection Policy
- The whistleblower protection policy is being implemented at [your company] to comply with the Public Company Accounting Reform and Investor Protection Act of 2002 (Sarbanes-Oxley).
- At [your company], any employee who reports waste, fraud, or abuse will not be fired or otherwise retaliated against for making the report.
- The report will be investigated, and even if determined not to be waste, fraud, or abuse, the individual making the report will not be retaliated against. There will be no punishment for reporting problems—including firing, demotion, suspension, harassment, failure to consider the employee for promotion, or any other kind of discrimination.

Methods for Reporting Waste, Fraud, or Abuse
There are several ways your employees can report suspected waste, fraud, or abuse.

- Contact the company's ombudsman.
- Call the designated hotline that your company has set up for this purpose.
- Send an email to a designated address that your company has established for these types of reports.
- Make the report in writing and submit to the manager in charge of receiving these reports.

Investigating the Report
Your company would list the steps it would take to:

- Investigate the allegation.
- Disseminate the report findings, including to the person who filed the report.
- Take steps to deal with the issue addressed, including making operational or personnel changes.
- Contact law enforcement to deal with any criminal activities, if warranted.

employee morale. A whistleblower protection policy should serve to usher in a new environment of integrity and ethical behavior.

Communication is key to ensuring that all employees understand why reporting waste, fraud, and abuse is expected, what their rights are, and how investigations are conducted and findings presented. Every employee should be given a copy of the whistleblower policy; it should be made readily available for review in hard copy and electronic format; and it should be covered in any orientation or training programs the business offers to its employees. The company's legal counsel should review the wording of the whistleblower protection policy and provide advice whenever whistleblower reports are filed.

Step 5: How Do You Make Sure the SOPs Are Effective?
Once the policy is in place, management should take steps to determine whether:

- All employees know how to report waste, fraud, or abuse. Are procedures in place to investigate reports, including how the person reporting will be advised of the outcome of the investigation?
- Privacy protocols are in place to protect confidential personnel information.
- Individuals who make reports are protected against any kind of mistreatment. Management should routinely contact individuals who make reports to determine if their experience was positive or they encountered any negative feedback.

A whistleblower protection policy is one of the most important steps you can take to safeguard your company. Unfortunately, many small businesses resist active implementation and enforcement of whistleblower protection because they are afraid of the implications of someone blowing the whistle on waste, fraud, and abuse, particularly if the company is family-owned. In truth, you owe it to yourself, your employees, and your customers to rise about these fears and institute this valuable early-warning system. Use the whistleblower protection policy checklist provided in Exhibit 6.2 to make sure yours is effective.

DOCUMENT PRESERVATION POLICY

Like the whistleblower protection policy, the document preservation policy is an important means to help your company to grow and thrive.

Companies that don't have effective document management policies often find themselves in challenging, even disruptive, circumstances such as problems preparing tax returns or being called to respond to a tax audit. Instituting and maintaining an effective document management plan, which per SOX requirements contains a prohibition against the destruction of documents during an investigation or legal action, is one of the most important ways you can ensure the success of your company.

Here are some of the many benefits of instituting a solid document management program at your small business:

- *Ability to manage institutional knowledge.* Executives, managers, and employees know where specific documents and records are stored, and a method exists to facilitate immediate access. In addition, a set of protocols have been established for archiving documents and, at the appropriate time, destroying documents.

- *Assured compliance with SOX.* By means of instituting a policy prohibiting destruction of documents during an investigation or discovery, you ensure that everyone on the staff knows the proper handling of documents, as well as the penalties for failure to follow those guidelines.

- *Opportunities for continuous improvement.* Change—that is, continuous improvement—becomes an accepted element of technology applications. This enables the document management program to grow, expand, and improve with new technologies and methods.

- *Commitment to compliance.* Because document management is required under Sarbanes-Oxley, the enforcement of this policy in your company becomes an important signal to all employees that there will be no exceptions.

- *More effective employee performance reviews.* If an employee is not managing his or her documents per SOX requirements, it will be reflected in performance reviews. The employee will soon learn that his or her salary adjustments, or even continued employment, is contingent on the degree of compliance.

- *Improved results from auditors' reviews.* Your company's auditors will be examining the way documents (whether paper or electronic) are managed, and the way technology is used to facilitate SOX compliance. By developing your policy according to SOX requirements, you can rest assured of a good review from audits.

- *Improved performance.* The ability to access files instantly saves time and energy for everyone on the staff. Further, it brings about an efficiency of scale that translates into higher levels of productivity (Davis, 2005).

Ironically, Sarbanes-Oxley compliance standards reflect how companies should have been practicing document management. Having an integrated document management system ensures that important documents are stored in safe, accessible locations and are backed up on a daily basis. The core of any document management system is access and accountability. Having a solid document management program in place will introduce a higher level of efficiency and accountability. Each division will have individuals who are responsible for document preservation and whose performance review reflects how well they carry out these responsibilities.

As business operations have become increasingly dependent on technology applications and products, the role of IT has emerged as one of the key operational units within any company or company. The executive team is tasked with ensuring that SOX compliance and best practices are implemented, but it is the IT division that will execute the assignment.

Using the Blueprint to Create an Effective Document Preservation Policy

Your company may already have a system in place to track documents. If that's the case, you have a head start on the process. The SOX requirements will serve to help you upgrade your current system. Specifically, if your current system does not include a prohibition against the destruction of documents during an investigation and/or legal proceedings, you will need to add one.

As with the whistleblower protection policy, here we will rework the Blueprint steps as a series of questions, to guide you in the formulation of your document preservation policy.

Step 1: How Would You Define Your Company's Style and Culture?
As part of your company's document management program, you, the owner, along with your senior management, are responsible for setting the tone when you announce its implementation, emphasizing its importance, as well as your commitment to ongoing enforcement. Leave no doubt in anyone's mind that compliance with the company's document preservation policy is a condition of their continued employment. Delegate responsibilities and assign accountability appropriately—this is essential to the effectiveness of any document management program—and maintain communication throughout the company on an ongoing basis.

**Step 2: What Could Damage Your Company's Operations
or Reputation?**
As with the whistleblower policy, failing to put an effective document preservation policy in place at your company could have dire consequences, perhaps even criminal prosecution. More likely, however, the absence of a document preservation policy will hamper any investigations and cause unnecessary problems and expense for the company.

Step 3: What Are Your Standard Operating Procedures?
Implementing a document preservation system at your company need not be a daunting process. Start by assembling a cross-functional team representing each division within your company. Each member of the team should be named as his or her functional area's document manager, in charge of coordinating the document preservation policy components that apply to his or her department. It is essential to give all division managers the same training and education in company systems and technologies (scanners, software, and the like), to ensure that documents are selected, preserved, archived, and retrieved in a consistent, standardized manner. Establish rules for appropriate and secure electronic transmission of sensitive materials. Work with IT and legal professionals to ensure that these rules are comprehensive and appropriate to your small business. And don't forget to have your legal counsel review and approve the actual language of your policy, in particular the prohibition against the destruction of documents during investigations.

EXHIBIT 6.3   SAMPLE MINIMUM STORAGE
REQUIREMENTS

Document	Storage
Accounts receivable and payable ledgers	7 years
Articles of incorporation, charter, bylaws, minutes	Permanently
Bank reconciliation	3 years
Bank statements, electronic fund transfers, and canceled checks	3 years
Contracts, mortgages, notes, and leases (expired)	7 years
Deeds, mortgages, and bills of sale	Permanently
Payroll records	7 years
Contracts still in effect	Permanently
Correspondence—legal	Permanently
Correspondence—vendors	2 years
Tax returns and worksheets	Permanently
Grants (funded)	7 years after closure

Source: National Association of Veterans Research and Education Foundations

Ask your legal counsel, financial professional, and/or IT professional to oversee the development of document retention rules (based on legal requirements and the operational needs of your small business) and follow up by disseminating these rules to all employees. You should have a security classification system. Keep it simple, for example, classifying documents as "confidential," "private," or another designation that precludes them from general access. Review and approve rules for managing, storing, preserving, and archiving electronic messages or other electronic data. The rules should address the important issues, which include detailing the types of documents to be retained and how these documents are to be stored.

Other issues to address in your document preservation policy:

- Who is the person to contact when looking for a specific type of record?

- Who is the go-to person for document preservation and to locate records in every department of your company? Will every department in your company have such a person, or will one individual be responsible for this overall?

EXHIBIT 6.4   DOCUMENT PRESERVATION POLICY AND STORAGE PROTOCOLS WORKSHEET

Document Preservation Policy: Talking Points

Key questions to answer in a document perservation policy include:

- Why does your small business need a document preservation and storage policy?
  It's required by the Public Company Accounting Reform and Investor Protection Act of 2002 (Sarbanes-Oxley).
- What documents and records should be preserved and why?
  See list of documents below.
- Why is there a rule against document destruction? When should you not destroy materials?
  If an official investigation is under way or even anticipated, small business management must stop any document purging in order to avoid criminal obstruction charges.

Writing the Policy: Talking Points

What is the document preservation and storage policy and why is it required by law? It's not just a "best practice"; it's the law and it applies to all organizations in this country. Your small business has an obligation to your customers, your clients, your board, and your staff to ensure that your organization is in compliance with this component of Sarbanes-Oxley legislation.

How does it work? In this section of the policy, provide your employees with some clear guidelines. (Emphasize the important issues. The guidelines should not be voluminous. If your guidelines are more than 10 pages, consider if all of the information is necessary.)

The guidelines should answer the questions:
- How do I start?
- What should my files look like when I'm finished?
- How long do I have to do this?
- What files should I ensure are retained and stored (this will be discussed in the next section).
- When should I *not* destroy files? When an instruction is sent to everyone at [your small business] to stop document destruction. You are expected to stop destroying documents until you receive an instruction stating that document destruction can resume. The small business's Document Preservation Policy needs to include a policy that prohibits destruction of documents during a regulatory or legal investigation.

Include these talking points:

- When are employees prohibited from destroying files? When an instruction is sent to everyone to stop document destruction.

- Employees are expected to stop destroying documents until such time that they receive an instruction stating that document destruction can resume.
- Employees must always receive permission before documents in any of the document preservation categories are destroyed.
- How do we maintain files and determine which are sent to storage? Also, discuss when files can be destroyed (after *X* number of years—depending on the type of file—and not when a moratorium is in place).
- Documents: Not all of these document categories are applicable to your small business, so only include the ones that are, and add those special document categories that your small business needs (but might not have been on the list). Be sure to include a brief description of these documents that would be meaningful to the employees at your small business.

Types of Documents to Store/Archive and Be Able to Retrieve:

- Financial documents, reports, analyses, and forecasts
- Customer records, history, and correspondence
- HR records
- Documents that reflect the sale of property, merchandise, or any tangible or intangible assets
- Documents that a regulatory agency or the law requires you to retain, such as tax returns, business license documents, professional licenses, vehicle registration forms, and correspondence regarding these documents or about your small business's operations
- Documents containing information that an auditor or regulator would need to review
- Contracts with vendors for services, including insurance policies, auditor contracts (particularly to demonstrate that the auditing firm is not providing any other services to your small business)
- Contracts with external clients (such as public sector agencies) to provide services to these external clients
- Client files and correspondence
- Customer files and correspondence with customers
- Proposals in response to proposals and/or bids
- Documents related to your small business's operations
- Instant messages or emails that contain negotiations for a contract or other legal agreement
- Business transactions: Any document that would provide proof that your small business took action in a business, contractual, or legal matter
- Special designations for sensitive documents

Design a *simple* classification system that allows for some of the documents to be classified as "confidential," "private," or other designation that precludes them from general access.

Storing and Archiving the Documents

The rules for managing, storing, preserving, and archiving electronic messages or other electronic data should address the important issues, including listing the types of documents that are to be retained and how these documents are to be stored. The rules should also include steps to be taken to ensure that the documents cannot be tampered with, such as using PDF files or passwords. It is particularly important to store financial

EXHIBIT 6.4   *(CONTINUED)*

records in such a way as to ensure that they represent a true and honest picture of the small business's financial profile and/or other financial description. Regulators will expect to be able to rely on the accuracy of all of your electronic records—no exceptions.

Testing the System
Develop a means by which the document preservation system will be tested on a regular basis to ensure that documents are stored properly and, more importantly, can be retrieved quickly. Employees should understand that the audits will be random and unannounced. There should be consequences for noncooperation, which should be meted out quickly to send a message to the entire organization.

- How will vendors handle your files? If you outsource a function, such as payroll, your policy needs to instruct the vendors how they are expected to manage your company's documents. Allow for no deviation.

As noted previously, implementing a document management program need not be overwhelming. It does, however, have to address what is *necessary and sufficient;* and the requirements need to be easy to understand and user-friendly—that is, easy to carry out. See Exhibit 6.3, which itemizes how long you need to store documents, and Exhibit 6.4, a worksheet to help you in formulating your company's document management program.

To begin, make note of the following categories of documents shown in Exhibit 6.4 that should be retained. These categories of documents have the following characteristics:

- Documents relating to financial transactions
- Documents that trace relationships with clients
- Documents that trace business transactions such as the sale or purchase of goods, services, or property
- Documents that relate to the company's human resources
- Documents that are part of legal proceedings or are required by law or regulation
- Documents that the company's auditors would require

Design your document management system so that it is logical and easy to use. If employees can't understand what's expected of them and why, then the system's probability of success will be low. Follow these guidelines:

- Build in the requirements of any third-party reviewers such as auditors or regulatory agencies, so that your system satisfies their expectations.

- Develop a process for finding and preserving any documents that either will be or are already evidence in an investigation or legal action. Include a statement that no documents are to be destroyed until an "all clear" notice is given. State the penalties for failing to adhere to this directive.

- Develop rules for managing, storing, preserving, and archiving electronic messages or other electronic data. List the types of documents that are to be retained and how these documents are to be stored. The process need not be complicated, but the rules need to be standardized—no "doing your own thing." The rules should include the steps to take to ensure that the documents cannot be tampered with—such as using PDF files or passwords. It is particularly important that financial records are stored in such a way to ensure that they represent a true and honest picture of the small business's financial profile and/or other financial description. Regulators will expect to be able to rely on the accuracy of all of your electronic records—no exceptions.

- Inventory the company's current record system to determine what records are in use, in storage, and archived. Include a review of the types of email messages and instant messages that are routinely transmitted, along with attachments. Establish rules for appropriate and secure electronic transmission of sensitive materials. Work with IT and legal professionals to ensure that these rules are comprehensive and appropriate to your company.

- Establish retention rules based on legal requirements and the operational needs of your company. Clearly disseminate these rules to all employees. Classify documents as "confidential," "private," or

EXHIBIT 6.5 TECHNOLOGY POLICY CHECKLIST

- All components of the company's technology belongs to the company. There are *no* expectations of personal privacy when using the company's technology.
- Email and Web access belong to the company.
- Examples of inappropriate email messages:
  - Jokes
  - Harassment
  - Political commentary, particularly hate messages
  - Anything you wouldn't want to read on the front page of your local newspaper, or have CNN broadcast
- The policy covers all of the company's technology – hardware and software including laptop computers and desktop computers, hand-held devices such as PDAs and BlackBerry devices, and cell phones; Internet access and email; and all software programs purchased through the company.
- Require return of all electronic devices such as laptops or PDAs when leaving the employ.
- Policy on the storage and transportation of sensitive information on laptops that leave your premises.
- Employees who are entrusted with the company's cell phones, laptops, PDAs, or other electronics need to understand that they will be held personally accountable for the safety of the equipment, the safe use of the equipment, and the security of the data that is stored within these electronics.

other designation that precludes them from general access. Launch a training program for employees to ensure that they understand what is expected of them, what the procedures are, and what records they are expected to retain.

Technology Policy as a Component of Document Preservation

It will come as no surprise to you that your company's technology policy (introduced in Chapter 3) is an important component of document preservation. Exhibit 6.5 contains a technology policy checklist, and the following guidelines supplement that information.

- *Store and archive all of the materials relating to employee briefings.* In personnel files, include copies of the letters signed by employees acknowledging their receipt of a written copy of the document management policy and agreeing to be in compliance. In the absence of personnel files, scan these letters for storage in the company database.

- *Develop a working inventory of all of the company's technologies.* Update this information on a daily or weekly basis, as necessary. The inventory should include hardware and software, including laptop and desktop computers; hand-held devices such as PDAs and BlackBerry devices, and cell phones; Internet access and email programs; and all software programs purchased through the small business. Be aware that when electronic devices such as laptops or PDAs are "recycled" to another employee member, the hard drives may still contain data, documents, or transactions from the previous employee. It is important to institute a procedure to erase the hard drive once all of the documents have been extracted and stored according to your company's document retention policy.

- *Draft a policy on how to store and transport sensitive information outside of your small business's facilities.* We've all read the stories of laptops containing client financial data being stolen. The same thing could happen to your small business if you store sensitive information about customers, clients, or employees on laptops that leave company premises.

- *Include a policy statement regarding the surrender of company property.* This states, in effect, that when employees leave the firm they will be expected to surrender all company technology to the HR department prior to departure, for which they will be given a signed receipt from HR.

- Establish rules for appropriate and secure electronic transmission of sensitive materials. Work with IT and legal professionals to ensure that these rules are comprehensive and appropriate to your small business.

Privacy Policy as a Component of Document Preservation

How is sensitive information about clients and employees handled and managed at your company? Does your small business have a privacy policy? If not, you need to institute one immediately, and disseminate it to both constituencies. For example, if your small business has a Web site, do you include a list of current and former clients? Before listing

EXHIBIT 6.6	SAMPLE POLICY: PROHIBITION AGAINST DESTROYING DOCUMENTS

The company's document preservation policy needs to include a policy that prohibits destruction of documents during a regulatory or legal investigation.
  Talking points:

- When are employees prohibited from destroying files? When an instruction is sent to everyone to stop document destruction.
- Employees are expected to stop destroying documents until such time that they receive an instruction stating that document destruction can resume.
- Employees must always receive permission before destroying documents in any of the document preservation categories.

these names, did you obtain a signed consent document from each of these clients? In today's world of identity theft and Internet hacking, it is vital to protect everyone involved with your firm. Simply put, you cannot be too careful.

SOP on Prohibition of Destruction of Documents

As you know by now, the primary SOP of your document management program is to design a process for preserving documents that either will be or are part of an investigation or legal action. The "talking points" of this SOP are itemized in Exhibit 6.6. Furthermore, you must have a mechanism for announcing that such documents are not to be destroyed until an "all clear" notice is given, and that stiff penalties will apply to those failing to adhere to this directive. If an official investigation is under way or even anticipated, company management must ensure that all document purging stops, in order to avoid criminal obstruction charges. Sarbanes-Oxley legislation is clear about the requirement to provide investigators with any and all documents necessary for an investigation. This means that your company, and its IT division, has to be able to retrieve relevant documents in a timely fashion.

To ensure compliance, draft a *brief* policy statement, using simple language, prohibiting the destruction of documents while the company is part of an investigation or other crisis scenario. It should just state that in the event of an investigation or crisis, there will be a general order circulated to prohibit the destruction of any documents. Describe the consequences for failure to comply with this policy, and have your attorney review and approve the language before you circulate it.

Important! It is essential that your company be prepared to impose the penalties it states in a policy like this. If not, don't include language to that effect.

Step 4: How Can You Ensure Everyone Is on the Same Page?
The quality of training in document management is critical to the success of the system. Too often, the reason people do not treat management directives seriously is because they do not receive adequate training; nor is there any follow-through or explanation of how the changes affect them personally. In other words, employees do not understand that they have an individual responsibility for complying with the directives, and that the quality of their compliance will be assessed at their next performance evaluation. The point is, enforcement of document management compliance must be consistent and made a condition of employment.

To that end, the owner(s) and senior management need to issue a policy statement on document preservation that answers the following questions:

- What does the document retention policy entail and why is it required by law? It is important that the employees understand that document preservation is a component of SOX that applies to all companies.
- What are the new procedures resulting from the policy? What are the deliverables that management expects?
- What does this legal requirement mean for the company?
- What are the obligations of individual employees to ensure that the company is in compliance?
- What is expected in terms of new behaviors and procedures? What are the consequences for failing to adhere to the new procedures?

Step 5: How Do You Make Sure the SOPs Are Effective?

One of the most important features of the policy are the routine audits of the document retention system, generally on an unannounced basis. The findings of these audits will provide the document retention team with valuable insight into the quality of the current protocols, the degree to which employee members are in compliance, and the modifications necessary to achieve full compliance.

You, as owner, and your management team will need to develop a means by which the document preservation system will be audited, on a regular and ongoing basis, to ensure that all employees are in compliance with its provisions. There are three primary categories of audits:

1. *External audit.* An outside consultant assesses the program. The company brings in an individual from outside the company to review and assess the current program.

2. *Internal audit.* The management team or their representatives do a spot-check of individuals to see if their records are in compliance. If not, the failure is documented and included in the employee's performance review. Noncomplying employees may be subject to penalties.

3. *Record categories.* As part of a spot-check, the reviewer determines where particular records should be located and checks to see if they are where they should be.

The results of the ongoing auditing and monitoring processes should be reviewed to determine whether additional enforcement measures are necessary to bring about standardized results. The program should also contain a continuous improvement aspect to ensure that new processes are adapted to achieve further efficiencies and effectiveness (Kohn, 2004).

NEXT STEPS

This chapter provided a step-by-step review of how to use the Blueprint to streamline the activities for implementation of both whistleblower protection and document preservation. These SOX requirements provide your company with two very important safe-guards: (1) an early-warning system to report waste, fraud, or abuse; and (2) the preservation and security of documents, vital to the well-being of your company. In Chapter 6, we will examine how the Blueprint can be used to facilitate the implementation of SOX best practices.

CHAPTER 7

The Blueprint and SOX Best Practices

This emphasis of this chapter is on developing a coherent approach to improving internal controls using the Blueprint. Benefits of implementation of best practices include strengthening the business infrastructure, improving efficiency, and serving as a marketing tool. SOX compliance and best practices also can be leveraged to differentiate the business from its competitors and to qualify it for access to attractive business ventures and collaborative partners.

In Chapter 4 we examined an array of best practices that emerged from Sarbanes-Oxley legislation. As noted, these best practices have become the gold standard in business management for companies that are not publicly traded. To review, the best practices include:

- *Upgrading the current quality of audits by means of auditor independence and an audit committee.* The individual who conducts the company's audit should not be providing any other services to the company, such as tax preparation or consulting. If the company has a board, the executive committee needs to appoint an audit committee whose role is to oversee the annual audit or financial review (for small businesses) and to upgrade the financial literacy of management and corporate board.

- *Ensuring accuracy of certified financial statements.* The management in any small business is ultimately accountable for the accuracy and integrity of the company's financial statements and tax return. The company needs to ensure that the CEO or CFO can validate the accuracy of the business's financial statements

- *Instituting a higher level of management accountability.* This includes upgrading policies and procedures for management accountability, adding new management orientation, and specifying performance expectations.

- *Establishing a conflict of interest policy.* This policy will apply to the company board (if there is one), managers, and employees to facilitate as sharper focus on decision-making processes, for the good of the business.

- *Developing a code of ethics.* This code must apply to the company board (if there is one), managers, and employees. It should preclude any loans to directors, officers, managers, or employees of the business. The code of ethics should also address gifts or other potential "kickbacks" from vendors.

- *Implementing internal controls.* In particular, these relate to financial operations and to compliance with all laws and regulations at the federal, state, and local levels.

- *Segregating duties* to ensure that employees have distinct duties related to finance or handling of other assets to reduce the potential for manipulation or fraud.

- *Recognizing the role of technology in the company's internal controls.* Your company's technology system serves as the framework for ensuring that internal controls are in compliance. Your auditor can assist in identifying any flaws in your company's processes or internal controls. Once these have been identified, it is imperative to remedy them at once, even if it means acquiring additional resources (Van Orden, 2004).

- *Ensuring transparency at all levels of management and in all transactions.* This includes all travel claims and reimbursements.

- *Assuring consistent adherence to and enforcement of new policies and procedures.* Management will not be successful in its endeavors to bring the business into SOX compliance unless the new policies and procedures are stringently enforced.

USING THE BLUEPRINT TO IMPLEMENT SOX BEST PRACTICES

The Blueprint is a useful tool for organizing the actions necessary to implement best practices. If your company does not have these best practices in place, it's a good idea to implement them in a sequential fashion. Doing so helps to minimize the amount of work necessary to introduce the practices, at the same time you maintain a steady pace of progress.

As in previous chapters, we'll use the five steps of the Blueprint reformulated as questions to explain how to implement the best practices. And for the sake of simplicity, the best practices are addressed as a group.

Step 1: What's Your Company's Style and Culture?

Your company's culture is an important factor in deciding how to go about introducing SOX best practices. You need to ask how can you leverage the best aspects of your company culture to implement SOX best practices, particularly internal controls. You will also need to consider whether there are some aspects of the culture that will need to change. If there are, be aware that SOX best practices themselves can very well serve to help you make these changes automatically, in terms of new behavior. But perhaps the most important thing to consider is how you, as the owner or senior manager of the company, plan to model the desired behavior. No one else will take the changes seriously until and unless they see management practicing what they preach.

The first step is to decide on a strategy for introducing change and modeling the new behavior at the top. To do this, begin by identifying the most notable aspects of your company's culture. Perhaps it's the "big happy family" atmosphere, which helps you to retain good employees. Or it's your company's compensation package, which provides family-friendly benefits and alternative types of work arrangements. Maybe it's that your company rewards positive behaviors on a regular basis, at the same time it metes out fair penalties for negative behaviors. You'll also want to consider how you can leverage the company's "star players" as a type of social marketing tool to promote the changes to their peers.

As you go about this investigation into your company culture, be realistic about those aspects you want to change, and be prepared to openly discuss these aspects as you introduce the SOX-related changes and articulate the desired behavior.

Step 2: What Could Damage Your Company's Operations or Reputation?

The next step is to imagine how not introducing these best practices could impact your business. Your findings here will be important when it's time to frame the discussion on SOX implementation with your employees. The following are examples of risk issues that, if left unaddressed, could damage your company's operations or reputation within the context of the best practices:

- *Auditor independence.* As stated previously, the person or firm who conducts the company's audit should not be providing any other services to the company, such as tax preparation or consulting. You, as the owner, and/or senior management also need to work quickly to address any issues that are reported in the auditor's management letter. If the company has a board, you'll need an audit committee. (Note: The section later in the chapter on establishing SOPs will provide additional information on the structure and function of this important committee.)

- *Certified financial statements.* As stated earlier, the company's owner(s) and/or managers are ultimately accountable for the accuracy and integrity of the company's financial statements, as well as its tax return. Therefore, it's imperative that the CEO or CFO be able to validate the accuracy of the business's financial statements. Risk areas for your company include IRS audits and scrutiny by other regulators. It's important to point out that if your company's financials are unreliable, your firm will have difficulty accessing capital, getting insurance, and, possibly, forming other business collaborations. Merger and acquisition (M&A) opportunities could be lost because of your company's unreliable books.

- *Management accountability.* The biggest risk of not implementing SOX best practices is that without a visible change in management accountability, the rank and file of your firm will resist or even ignore implementing these necessary best practices in their day-to-day operations. Without upgraded policies and procedures for management accountability, new management orientation, and performance expectations, your company puts itself at risk for fraud and misappropriation of assets.

- *Conflict of interest policy.* Without an effective conflict of interest policy in place, managers and employees alike may, for a variety of reasons, be tempted to engage in unethical practices, such as contracting with businesses in which they have an interest or relationship, simply because your company no direct prohibition against doing so. Having a conflict of interest policy is particularly important if your company has a board of directors. Each board member should be required to sign an affidavit on a yearly basis that discloses real or potential conflicts of interest. Keep in mind, your company could be subject to criminal prosecution for accepting kickbacks or other engaging in any activities contrary to the policy. The resultant negative publicity could damage your business, making it less attractive to potential customers and vendors, prospective employees, or prospective board members.

- *Code of ethics.* It's notable that many of the companies and nonprofits that have been involved in recent financial scandals have loaned money to senior management or board members. Your company needs to have a means of prohibiting or discouraging any loans to directors, officers, managers, or employees of the business, except under the strictest of conditions. Your banker, auditor, or legal counsel can advise you as to when it might be appropriate to authorize and manage such loans. The code of ethics should also specifically prohibit the acceptance of gifts or other potential "kickbacks" from vendors.

- *Internal controls.* If your company has few or weak internal controls, it is at risk for embezzlement, misappropriation of resources, or other types of fraud. Further, your company is seen as a poor candidate for acquisition and a high risk when you want to access capital or insurance markets. For example, your bank may charge you a higher interest rate for a line of credit, or decline to offer you other sources of funds at competitive terms.

- *Failure to recognize the role of technology in your company's internal controls.* This oversight can set up a barrier impeding the upgrade of your current internal audits. It is important to recognize that system changes are required to meet compliance guidelines. You will need to make them immediately, so be prepared to sign on additional help if your internal resources are insufficient. The quality of your company's IT systems can either facilitate or bog down implementation of these best practices. Further, a strong IT structure is essential to reduce the potential of hackers and other external sources compromising your proprietary data, particularly confidential customer information such as credit card numbers. Publicity surrounding such a breach could have long-lasting negative effects on your company, including loss of customers and venture partners.

- *Transparency at all levels of management and in all transactions.* The flash points for risk issues surrounding management transparency often center on simple things such as inflated travel claims, use of company credit cards for personal expenses, and the extravagant use of expense accounts. In today's business environment, your company must demonstrate to all stakeholders that it has policies and procedures in place to ensure transparency, to combat such risk issues. This best practice can either enhance your company's competitive position or, by ignoring it, send the message that your company is a poor risk.

- *Consistent adherence to and enforcement of new policies and procedures.* Management will not be successful in its endeavors to bring the business into SOX compliance unless the new policies and procedures are enforced, and consistently. Failure to do so will mean that the time, effort, and money you invested to introduce the best practices was wasted. Your company cannot afford to have less than complete success in implementing SOX best practices.

Step 3: What Are Your Standard Operating Procedures?

If your company already has some of these best practices in place, have you identified specific ways employees are expected to perform? Are your SOPs documented and enforced? Here are examples of SOPs for each of the best practices.

Audits, Auditor Independence, and an Audit Committee

Auditor independence has become an important best practice. Selecting an auditor is an important step for your company, even if it does not have a board of directors and an audit committee.

Evaluating external auditors for the purpose of examining your company's financial statements is one of the primary responsibilities of senior management. If your company has a board, auditor selection should be done by the audit committee. A number of factors must be considered:

- Does the potential auditor have strong experience in the company's specialty area; does he or she understand the specific accounting requirements for the company?

- Does the potential auditor have a strong tax specialty in the company's industry sector?

- Does the potential auditor utilize information technology that is compatible with that used by the company? Will the auditor be able to access the company's electronic data with limited disruption?

- Does the potential auditor already provide accounting, consulting, or other services to the company, giving him or her a financial incentive to maintain the relationship at the expense of the audit?

- Does the potential auditor indicate that he or she will be able to work compatibly with, but independently of, the company's management team?

- Does the potential auditor understand that he or she will report directly to the audit committee, and not to management?
- Does the potential auditing firm have effective internal control policies? Are they periodically evaluated, and how?
- Does the potential auditing firm have effective recruitment, hiring, and employee training policies? How are they periodically evaluated?
- Does the potential auditing firm have sufficient personnel?
- Are the fees proposed by the potential auditing firm reasonable?

Again, the individual(s) who conduct the company's audit should not be involved in any other services provided to the company, such as tax preparation or consulting. If the company has a board, the executive committee needs to appoint an audit committee whose role is to oversee the annual audit or financial review and to upgrade the financial literacy of management and the corporate board. The value of having an audit committee is also reflected in the number of SOX provisions regarding the composition of the audit committee and its financial oversight duties in public companies. An effective audit committee should be responsible for the following tasks:

- Providing oversight of the internal control system
- Recommending an independent auditor to the board of directors
- Reviewing the overall of plan of the audit
- Reviewing the results of the audit with the external auditor
- Reporting the audit findings to the full board

In essence, the role of the company's audit committee is to oversee, monitor, and work collaboratively with management to prepare financial statements and conduct internal audits of those statements. The committee also must oversee, monitor, and work collaboratively with external auditors in conducting audits. In light of the many corporate and company financial scandals, the audit committee must perform this role in a proactive manner. The audit committee needs to safeguard the overall objectivity of the financial statements, financial reporting, and the internal controls process. To do so, the audit committee should ensure that effective internal control processes have been developed and fully implemented by management and employees. In addition, the audit committee should ascertain that all employees and managers involved in the financial reporting and internal controls process understand their roles, and that they are fulfilling those roles. The audit committee also should work closely with external auditors to identify and analyze financial reporting problems, and then use that information to make policy recommendations to management and the rest of the board.

To reiterate, the best practices presented here are intended to institute a higher level of management accountability, which includes certifying financial statements and upgrading policies and procedures for management accountability, new management orientation, and performance expectations. Remember, the company's management is ultimately accountable for the accuracy and integrity of its financial statements, as well as its tax return, so the CEO or CFO must be able to vouch for the accuracy of the business's financial statements.

Between 1987 and 1997, COSO examined 200 randomly selected cases of alleged financial fraud that were investigated by the SEC. Its primary findings, published in "Fraudulent Financial Reporting: 1987–1997—An Analysis of U.S. Public Companies" (1999), were:

- Senior managers were frequently involved. In 83 percent of the cases, the chief executive officer, the chief financial officer, or both were associated with the financial statement fraud.

- Most fraud was not limited to a single fiscal period; the fraud was ongoing, perpetrated over several fiscal periods, with an average fraud period of 23.7 months.

- The majority of the fraud schemes involved the overstatement of revenues and assets.

- Most fraud occurred in smaller companies (with assets less $100 million), but the average amount of fraud was relatively large ($25 million).

These findings point to SOPs in key areas of financial controls that are essential to ensuring that the CEO and CFO can certify that the company's financials are accurate. These key areas are:

- Cash receipts
- Cash disbursements
- Accounts receivable
- Accounts payable
- Petty cash
- Segregation of duties
- Check signing
- Payment documentation
- Inventory
- Employee advances
- Employee travel
- Payroll
- Fixed assets
- Bank statement reconciliation
- Fund management

Cash Receipts

The category of cash receipts encompasses issuance of receipts, acceptance of cash and deposits, and recording of cash in any form; and includes currency and checks. Financial controls help to ensure that all cash intended for the company is received, promptly deposited, properly recorded and reconciled, and kept under adequate security.

Cash Disbursements

For an effective financial control of any cash disbursements it is essential to develop policies whereby different people authorize payments, sign checks, record payments in books, and reconcile the bank statements. It is important also to certify that cash disbursements are made under proper authorization and for valid business reasons and are recorded properly.

Accounts Receivable

Accounts receivables are amounts owned to the company from sales or delivery of services to its clientele made on credit. Adequate accounts receivable controls include properly recording payments and arranging for quick recoveries of payments. Recovery efforts should escalate if there is any delay in the recovery process. Parties that continue to be delinquent should be tracked and flagged for corrective action.

Accounts Payable

Accounts payables are amounts due from the company to suppliers or others goods or services rendered on credit. A proper financial control of accounts payable ensures that all invoices are legitimate and accurate and are properly paid and recorded.

Petty Cash

Petty cash is a fund maintained for payment for small incidental purchases or reimbursements. Many small businesses have a significant amount of petty cash on hand to meet everyday needs. However, dealing in cash represents a heightened degree of risk, thus a greater degree of care needs to be exercised. Proper controls of petty cash might include the following:

- Keep petty cash under lock and key.
- Determine a minimum and maximum amount to be kept in the fund at all times. There should be enough to cover petty cash expenditures for a month.
- Assign a limit on the amount of petty cash that can be disbursed at one time.
- Institute a process for petty cash disbursement.

Segregation of Duties

To exercise financial control best practices, your company should design an organizational structure to appropriately segregate responsibilities. Doing so reduces a person's opportunities to commit and conceal fraud or errors. It also allows for rotation of duties. Segregation essentially means that no one person will handle any financial transaction from beginning to the end. For example, in the case of paying invoices, one person should authorize the payment, another should draw the checks and record the payment in proper books of accounts, a third person should sign the checks, and a fourth person should reconcile the bank statements. With one individual given the ownership of his or her particular task, any break in the flow is immediately traceable.

Check Signing

A simple control regarding check signing requires checks to be signed by at least two different people, for amounts above a certain level. When different individuals are assigned the tasks of who to pay, how much to pay, why to pay, and when to pay, you create a check-and-balance on check signing, thereby making misappropriating funds difficult.

Payment Documentation

The proper control here is to support every payment by attaching the original invoice, with receipts and other documentation, to the invoice. When the payment is made by check, you should record the entry, along with the name of the person or firm to which payment was made, with the check number, check date, and check amount. Also record the names of the check signing authorities and obtain their signatures.

Inventory

Recommended internal controls for managing inventories of goods for sale or in stock include documenting all items; recording all deliveries, including the vendor name, product name and stock-keeping unit number, delivery date, shipment number, and quantity; and obtaining the shipment notice signed by the vendor. Compute beginning and ending stock on a daily basis and reconcile these statistics with sales numbers, to uncover any differences. If the company has a warehouse, staff there should be responsible for inventory numbers at that facility; in a store, the manager there should be responsible for sales and on-shelf inventories. Product returns should be tracked separately and authorized by a manager.

Employee Advances

Employee advances for anticipated expenses should be disbursed according to strict guidelines that, at a minimum, define the maximum cash amount that can be given to an employee; document the cash advance request; gain approval of the request before the cash advance is made; and, to close the loop, substantiate use of the cash. For example, an employee might receive a cash advance to purchase an office printer based on a quote. The transaction would close only after he or she submitted original receipts from the vendor, to make sure there are no differences in the quote, along with the final invoice, to safeguard against the employee returning the printer using the original receipt in exchange for something less costly.

Employee Travel

Control guidelines for employee travel include specifying modes of travel, giving travel notice, gaining travel approvals from managers, and justifying in writing the purpose of the travel. And when employees complete the travel arrangements, they must provide proper documentation in the form of original receipts and obtain a manager-approved form for reimbursement. Exhibit 7.1 contains a travel claims policy checklist.

Payroll

When it comes to payroll controls, it is necessary to ensure that payments are made only to bona fide employees for authorized amounts. Employees should be issued pay-slips showing their gross salary; all deductions, including tax and insurance; and their net salary. To avoid fraud or misuse of the company's funds, a separate payroll bank account should be maintained, and on a monthly basis, the payroll department should reconcile the net amounts on the pay-slips against the actual amounts paid by check. The payroll department should also keep salary and expense reimbursement accounts separate, for clarity.

Fixed Assets

Fixed assets are those that are not easily converted into cash in the short term—that is, within one year. They are long-term assets, both tangible and intangible, whose value extends beyond the accounting period.

EXHIBIT 7.1   TRAVEL CLAIMS POLICY CHECKLIST

- Travel claims are submitted on a specific form designed by the company. The form needs to capture the name of the employee, dates of travel, purpose of travel, listing of expenses, and documentation attached (original documentation should be required).
- The travel claim must indicate the purpose of the trip, the name of the person who authorized the travel, and a copy of the documentation.
- If the travel claim includes reimbursement for meals, the purpose of the meal and the names of the guests must be included. For example, if the meal was a business lunch while attending a conference, the receipt for the meal must be included and any guests or clients must be listed.
- If parking or transportation to the airport is an authorized expenditure, the travel claim also needs to have either a receipt for parking or a mileage listing.
- The company will specify the time frame within which a travel claim has to be filed, for example, within ten (10) business days of returning to the office.
- The travel expense policy includes a list of authorized expenditures. Any expenditures that are not included as authorized expenditures on the list must be approved by the CFO before they can be reimbursed.
- Travel claims will not be paid unless the form is completed correctly and there is supporting documentation for all expenses.
- Senior management will make random and unannounced examinations of travel claims within a specific time frame to ensure compliance.

Land, buildings, furniture and fixtures, and vehicles are examples of tangible assets, and goodwill, copyrights, licenses, and patents are examples of intangible fixed assets. Tangible fixed assets are recorded at their original cost and are depreciated proportionately every year, whereas intangible fixed assets are recorded at their original cost and are amortized proportionately every year.

The procedure for recording fixed assets includes proper tracking and control of the assets. Financial controls ensure that fixed assets are acquired and disposed of only with proper authorization, by taking adequate safety measures, and by properly recording the transactions. Also, due diligence should be performed and documented before any fixed asset is purchased, to ensure that the purchase amount paid is as agreed.

Bank Statement Reconciliation
Bank statement reconciliation is the process of systematically comparing the cash balance as reported by the bank with the cash balance on the

company's books and reconciling any differences between them. The balance on the bank statement, the checkbook balance, and the accounting book balance (the ledger and the journal) all must tally.

Fund Management or Funding
Without effective financial controls, a company runs the risk of consuming its funding faster than anticipated. It is therefore important to keep a close watch on how funds are raised and how, where, and why are they utilized.

Conflict of Interest Policy

The importance of having a conflict of interest policy in place at your company has been reiterated throughout this book. To restate, this policy facilitates proper decision-making procedures for both management and employees. Where a conflict of interest exists, either between a company employee and another person associated with the company, or between an employee and a vendor or stakeholder, there's a very real risk of legal problems. So an important aspect of this policy is to encourage everyone on your staff to disclose a suspected conflict of interest situation. It's also important to document any conflict of interest situation via a "Conflict of Interest Statement." All senior managers and key employees should submit this statement on an annual basis or in the event that a manager or key employee learns of a potential conflict of interest. And once a person has been implicated in a conflict of interest, he or she should be excused from participation in any company interactions where it would be inappropriate.

In addition to the talking points given in Exhibit 7.2, the following are some streamlined ways to introduce SOPs for managing a conflict of interest policy.

- The fiduciary obligations of management require them to put the financial interests of the company ahead of any personal gain. One way to ensure this is to identify those relationships and/or business dealings that either present a conflict of interest or have the potential for being a conflict of interest.

EXHIBIT 7.2   CONFLICT OF INTEREST POLICY
GUIDELINES

Does your company have a conflict of interest policy? If so, does it contain these talking points?

- Make it a legal standard of loyalty for management and key employees to put the financial interests of the company ahead of any personal gain. One way to achieve this is to identify those relationships and/or business dealings that either present a conflict of interest or have the potential for being a conflict of interest.
- Require that all employees sign a letter indicating real or potential conflicts of interest, or stating they have none. This way, the company has a record of those areas that may pose a conflict of interest for individual management and key employees. The company can then take steps to ensure that the individual managers and key employees do not take part in discussions or votes related to those areas.
- Ensure transparency and full disclosure, as they are very important in today's business environment.
- Explain the procedures to management and key employees for dealing with conflicts of interest so that they understand why it is essential that they disclose real or potential conflicts and what the procedures are for ensuring that decisions are made in an appropriate fashion.
- Require conflict of interest letters to be signed on an annual basis.
- When a discussion addresses an area that has been identified as a conflict of interest for someone, excuse the individual involved from the discussion; he or she must not permitted to vote. Record this in the minutes of the meeting.
- Reserve the right to ask an individual who presents a very serious conflict of interest to resign or be placed in a capacity that neutralizes the conflict.

Every manager and key employees should be required to sign a conflict of interest disclosure letter on an annual basis. The text of the letter should include these points:

I, [name of manager or key employee], state that I have/do not have the following personal, business, or professional relationships that may present a conflict of interest:
[type of conflict] I do not have any conflicts of interest.
[type of conflict] I have the following relationships or business interests that may pose a conflict of interest: [List those relationships and businesses that might pose as conflict of interest.]

As a member of [the name of the company], I commit to placing the company's interest and gain ahead of my own, and will further commit to excusing myself from any discussion or votes related to those areas in which I may have a conflict of interest.

Signed,
Date

- The company should require senior managers and key employees to sign a conflict of interest letter on an annual basis, identifying real or potential conflicts of interest, or stating that they have none. This gives the company a record of those areas that may pose a conflict of interest for individual managers and key employees. The company can then take steps to ensure that anyone implicated in a conflict of interest is prevented from taking part in discussions or votes related to, for example, the awarding of contracts or other actions that would be inappropriate.

- Transparency and full disclosure are very important in today's business environment. Therefore, the procedures for dealing with conflicts of interest must be explained clearly all employees, so that they understand why it is essential that they disclose real or suspected conflicts and what the procedures are for ensuring that decisions are made in an appropriate fashion.

- The company must reserve the right to ask any employee who presents a very serious conflict of interest to resign from its employ, or be placed in a capacity that neutralizes the risk.

The text of aforementioned conflict of interest disclosure letter should include the points covered in Exhibit 7.3. But be sure to have your

---

EXHIBIT 7.3   SAMPLE CONFLICT OF INTEREST LETTER LANGUAGE

I, [name of manager or key employee], state that I have/do not have the following personal, business or professional relationships that may present a conflict of interest:
   [type of conflict] I do not have any conflicts of interest.
   [type of conflict] I have the following relationships or business interests that may pose a conflict of interest: [List those relationships and businesses that might pose as conflict of interest.]
   As a member of [the name of the company], I commit to placing the company's interest and gain ahead of my own, and will further commit to excusing myself from any discussion or votes related to those areas in which I may have a conflict of interest.

Signed,
Date

company's legal counsel review and approve the actual wording of the letter before you ask your employees to sign it.

Code of Ethics

A company code of ethics is another important element of your SOPs. It should apply to managers and employees, alike, and the board of directors (if the company has one). All employees should be required to read, then sign, the code of ethics as acknowledgment that they agree to its terms. The code, as explained previously, should preclude any loans to directors, officers, managers, or employees of the business. It should also address gifts or other potential "kickbacks" from vendors.

The code of ethics needs to describe:

- The roles of senior managers and key employees, specifying ethical behavior expectations.

- The process for employees to raise ethical concerns, should they arise. One significant provision, as just noted, is the prohibition against any type of loan or financial gift by the company to a board member or employee at any level.

- The company's commitment to compliance with laws and regulations, accountability to the public, and the responsible handling of resources.

Other items to address in the company's code of ethics are organizational values, as expressed in the company's mission statement and other supporting documents, such as strategic plans.

Include:

- Mission
- Governance (if the company has a board)
- Legal compliance (the company's commitment to remain in compliance)

- Responsible stewardship of resources and financial oversight
- Openness and disclosure
- Professional integrity as related to all aspects of services rendered and in all business dealings
- Any other issues relating to your company operations

The following presents a sample code of ethics. Remember to have your company's legal counsel review and approve the actual wording of this document before you distribute it to your employees.

As a member of [the name of the company] I will:

Endeavor at all times to place the interest of [the name of the company] above my own personal interests.

Be diligent in the performance of my duties, come prepared to all meetings, and fulfill my obligations as a manager or key employee.

Seek to continually improve my knowledge of [the name of the company] and the industry sector.

Strive to establish and maintain integrity in my relationships with my superiors, colleagues, and subordinates at [the name of the company] and with the company's customers, vendors, and other stakeholders.

Strive to improve the public understanding of the mission and vision of [the name of the company].

Obey all laws and regulations and avoid any conduct or activity that would cause harm to [the name of the company].

Internal Controls

Internal controls are the "bones" of your company's operations. You will use them to monitor financial operations and compliance with all laws and regulations at the federal, state, and local levels. The company's commitment to adopting and maintaining SOX best practices can be demonstrated in a review of internal controls, the outcome of which can be used to measure the progress your company has made in the implementation of best practices. Compliance cannot be allowed to become a rote operation; it must be evident in practice on a daily basis that the commitment to excellence applies at all levels of the company and in all of the operational systems, including relationships that exist among the various systems within the company.

The internal controls of your company should work as the organs and pulmonary, nerve, and endocrine systems work in a human body. The synergy and interdependence of these systems are what keep a person alive and healthy. The dysfunction of one affects all the others. Thus, it is imperative to take a reading of your company's internal health by conducting a review of its internal controls. This means not just a review of financial systems but an examination of all of the systems within your company, from human resources to vendor selection, from document preservation to operations, and from landscaping to facilities maintenance.

The review of internal controls should center on the following functional areas.

Financial Operations

The examination of the systems and procedures associated with the finance department and overall financial operations is a primary element of the review of internal controls. This review is different from the company's annual financial audit in that it examines how financial operations are conducted, how transparent these operations are, and the relationship among the various other operational systems within the company. The review of internal controls should ascertain that the following procedures are in place:

- Processing incoming checks
- Preparing bank deposits
- Reconciling bank statements
- Disbursing cash and checks (A procedure should be in place to document these disbursements, requiring corresponding invoices or receipts for each transaction.)
- Recording transactions
- Actively monitoring credit cards and vendor accounts to ensure accuracy
- Putting a system in place to enable the confidential reporting of waste, fraud, and abuse

There should be more than one person handling the financial transactions. This can be achieved by having the company's controller work directly with the board treasurer (if one exists) to ensure adequate oversight.

Human Resources

Internal controls are essential for ensuring that complete personnel files exist for all employees and that their qualification to work (I-9) forms are complete and in order. These files should include job descriptions, contracts, time schedules, and any other documents or information pertinent to each employee, in particular compensation agreements. Recent court rulings have even highlighted the need to document the arrangement that your company has with workers regarding their lunch breaks and overtime.

You'll also need to specify for the Internal Revenue Service (IRS) which of your workers are company employees versus independent contractors, as these classifications have become a thorny issue. Why? If a person is classified as an independent contractor, the company is not liable for payroll taxes, worker's compensation, or unemployment insurance. So if your company is found to be improperly classifying certain of its employees as independent contractors, the IRS may exact sanctions against your firm in the form of unpaid employment taxes and insurance, along with, of course, stiff penalties.

In this era of heightened IRS scrutiny, it is equally important that your company classify staff employees accurately. The various factors the IRS uses to determine whether someone is an employee or independent contractor are listed in Exhibit 7.4.

Guidelines for Conducting a Review of Internal Controls

Step 1. Review the current practices in each of the company's functional areas, as outlined in the previous section. Identify the procedures that are currently in place.

Step 2. Document any SOX best practices currently in place at your company. Collect proof that your company is in compliance with

EXHIBIT 7.4	FACTORS DETERMINING EMPLOYEES VERSUS INDEPENDENT CONTRACTORS

Factor	Employee	Independent Contractor
Supervision	The worker must follow specific instructions on where, when, and how to perform the work.	The worker must produce a specified result, but is permitted to work at another location.
Schedule	Worker works full-time for one employer.	The worker works for more than one employer.
Workday	Employer defines how long the worker works per day.	The worker sets his or her own hours unless otherwise specified by engagement contract.
Location of work	Worker works exclusively on employer's premises.	Worker completes tasks at locations of his or her choice.
Assistants	Employer assigns assistants to worker.	Worker hires and supervises his or her own assistants.

Source: AllBusiness.com: The Advisor, 2005

the best practice. Examples include, but are not limited to, financial reports; written policies and procedures; enforcement procedures; documentation from third parties, such as an accrediting entity or an insurance company, stating that your company has implemented these practices; annual reports; and audits or annual financial reviews signed by a CPA or other financial expert.

Step 3. Assemble the examples of proof of SOX best practices compliance and/or appropriate internal controls.

Step 4. If you are unable to either identify a system that corresponds to a SOX best practice or a way to demonstrate proof of a SOX best practice, take these steps:

1. Identify the types of proof you would need. It might be a report, a set of policies and procedures, a written review, or action in the board minutes.

2. Determine the steps needed to develop the proof or set of procedures.

3. Develop time lines for obtaining the materials, as well as names of individuals responsible for meeting deadlines.

Content and Structure of the Review of Internal Controls Report

- *Introduction:* The introduction, a statement from the board (if your company has one) and senior management, explains why the audit is taking place and the expected deliverables from the audit.

- *Systems:* For each department provide a brief description of each of the protocols, procedures, and/or systems, then compare them with recommended internal controls and SOX best practices and expectations: The following areas are examples of departments:
  - Finance
  - Document retention
  - HR
  - Operations
  - Governance
  - Other areas of the company

- *Next steps and deliverables:* The discussion in this section addresses remedial action that will be taken to upgrade current operational systems so that they comply with SOX best practices. It is important to clearly identify these deliverables.

- *Timeline:* Here you establish a reasonable timeline for addressing the deliverables identified in the previous section. Decide what you would intend to accomplish in one month, three months, and six months. Set a deadline for completing all of the systems/proof by 10 months from the start of the project. A word of warning: Don't set too long a time frame or you risk the project becoming lost in the everyday shuffle of operations. Finally, book a "look back" date at the end of the 10-month period to determine if additional work is needed.

- *Statement of transparency at all levels of management and commitment to adherence to and enforcement of new policies and procedures.* Management will not be successful in its endeavors to bring the company into SOX compliance unless the new policies and procedures are enforced. Having strong internal controls facilitates transparency at all levels, and enforcement protocols ensure that everyone in the company will be held accountable for their behavior.

Step 4: How Do You Ensure Everyone Is on the Same Page?

To come into full compliance, it is essential that all employees and managers understand what is expected of them. Introducing a series of new policies, procedures, and practices can be confusing, hence become frustrating, unless you cover the following talking points and review them on a regular basis:

- Define the new practice—be specific.

- Explain why the new practice is being put in place. Don't just say, "It's the law." Detail how and why the new practice will protect your company, and don't be shy about using the words "fraud" or "misappropriation." The company may not have experienced a fraud-related crisis yet, and the implementation of these best practices will lower the potential for one happening.

- Describe your role. How you are going to change your behavior to ensure compliance? If you expect your employees to take the changes seriously, you'll have to be the role model.

- Explain what you expect from your employees in terms of performance and quality. Be specific. As a follow-up measure, repeat what you said in writing, so that employees have resource material for referral.

- Describe to employees that how well they adopt these new practices will be evaluated. Detail the consequences for noncompliance and/or failure to cooperate.

Step 5: How Do You Make Sure the Sops Are Effective?

Conducting an internal audit is an effective way of checking on the level of compliance with SOX requirements and best practices. Unannounced audits are particularly effective, as they can produce a real-time snapshot of your company's operations. You can also attach specific metrics to each of the best practices to identify compliance levels and to determine whether the current SOPs are effective. It's also important to test IT systems and procedures, to give managers and key administrators insight into the quality of systems integration.

NEXT STEPS

Your company can leverage its efforts to implement SOX requirements and best practices by applying what you have learned in the development of a risk management program and business continuity plan. Your commitment to SOX compliance can also pay dividends in the form of strengthening and enriching your company's relationships with its professional advisors, such as bankers, insurance professionals, IT professionals, payroll vendors, and legal counsel. Chapter 8 will examine how you can expand the benefits of SOX compliance to further strengthen your company.

Adding Value to SOX Requirements and Best Practices

The client appeared nervous and distracted. Having worked with this woman before, her demeanor seemed unusual. The consultant asked if anything was troubling her and she replied that the thought of assembling an entire risk management plan was daunting. The consultant assured her that the first round of planning involved using an outline. As she looked at the template, she exclaimed, "Fill in the blanks! I love it—this is going to work!"

This chapter will examine how your small business can leverage its SOX compliance and best practices to jump-start its risk management and business continuity planning, as well as improve its relationships with the professional experts it is already paying for. The benefits of working with these professionals more effectively are highly valuable. To start with, the partnerships become more productive, thus you gain enhanced value for their services; but just as important, you gain a deeper understanding of your company operations, as well as up-to-date knowledge of the latest outcomes of legal and legislative decisions and how they might affect you and your company.

HOW RISK MANAGEMENT AND BUSINESS CONTINUITY PLANNING RELATE TO SOX COMPLIANCE AND BEST PRACTICES

Risk Management

As discussed in Chapter 5, risk management is the means by which companies can identify, assess, and control risks that may be present within their business infrastructure or operations. The focus of much of SOX compliance and best practices is on the internal controls of the company, as well as the systems that the company has developed to enhance transparency and accountability. SOX best practices have a value-added component, in that they also identify how to mitigate risks associated with fiduciary obligations, legal compliance, board governance, and other areas of concern.

In contrast to the single-event implementation of SOX requirements and best practices, risk management is an ongoing process that works only when it is thoroughly integrated into the company's operations. Risk management activities focus on the quality of systems, behaviors, and changing expectations. A hallmark of good risk management practice is learning to adjust the company's best practices and ways of doing business to be congruent with current trends, expectations, relevant court decisions, and recent legislation. And for those companies that have boards, risk management emphasizes the quality of governance, including who is on the board, how the board interacts with management, how to avoid conflicts of interest, how to adhere to a code of conduct, and other best practices. Other aspects of risk management concentrate on workplace safety, adequate insurance coverage, and policies and procedures to safeguard the privacy of customers and employees alike.

Risk management acts, as does SOX, as an important deterrent to fraud. Like SOX, risk management activities point to the need to institute methods to report waste, fraud, and abuse. Early detection of fraud is critical for the economic viability and sustainability of the business. Thus, SOX practices to deter fraud should become part of an ongoing risk management plan.

Recognizing Legitimate Risk Management Practices

Although there are many techniques for managing risk available in the marketplace, it is important to be aware that some of these are *not* authentic risk management practices, although too often they are mistaken as such by misinformed individuals. The difference is in the results. Take note of the following practices that fail to produce a solid risk management plan, so that your company does not make this mistake:

- *Purchasing insurance from an agent or broker.* Insurance is a method for preventing risk, but it's not risk management. If employees in your company experience too many accidents, injuries, or other reasons to file claims, your insurance policy might be canceled, or the premium could increase so high that it becomes difficult or impossible to afford. Insurance covers only certain types of losses; it does not cover things such as punitive damages. Further, if your company has an adverse claims record and your insurance carrier cancels coverage, it may become difficult or impossible to obtain replacement coverage.

- *Setting up a committee for endless discussions on the topic.* Many companies, in an effort to obtain consensus on a topic, are prone to establish committees whose members engage in endless "study" or "discussion," with few meaningful results. Effective risk management committees, in contrast, assign deadlines and deliverables and hold people accountable.

- *Buying inappropriate software that only serves to address risk issues peripherally.* This practice is typically undertaken by individuals who have no interest in genuine risk management, but have been tasked with risk management planning. The software renders reports that are superficial at best. In terms of the objectives of good risk management practice, this is particularly dangerous, as the company may think it has a "risk management plan" in place, when in fact no one other than the person entering the data really has had any contact with it. This approach to risk management does nothing to educate your company's management and employees, nor does it help the board to understand what their obligations are in today's Sarbanes-Oxley compliance environment. Any product that allows your company to deal with risk management at an arm's length does not provide value for the money.

- *Playing it by ear and hoping for the best.* As the saying goes, "Denial isn't a river in Egypt." Risk management isn't something that your company can endlessly defer because it just doesn't have the time to deal with it right now. A prospective client once told me that she felt risk management activities were a "luxury" that took up valuable time her company needed to spend on marketing!

- *Pleading ignorance—"No one told us we had to do something about risk."* Some companies ignore professionals who tell them that they need to engage in risk management activities. Your company's obligation to manage risk should stem from its commitment to its mission. That is, no one should have to tell you to engage in risk management or business continuity planning; your firm should be eager to embrace this type of planning to ensure its ongoing viability.

Now that we've examined some types of activities that are not genuine risk management, let's look at the clues indicating a company has a solid risk management program in place:

- *Everyone is on the same page.* From the owner to the mailroom clerk to the newest hire, everyone on staff understands what risk management is and what their role is in the company's risk management plan. They also recognize they will be rewarded for compliance and, conversely, penalized for failing to comply. The board and senior management models the desired behavior, and all employees are actively engaged in risk management practices. In sum, risk management is part of the company's standard operating procedures.

- *Risk management is an ongoing process.* Once a risk management plan is in place, planning is an ongoing process, with rounds having a three- to six-month cycle. Everyone in the company has a copy of the current risk management plan and knows what is expected of them.

- *The company partners with its external advisors.* Genuine risk management planning includes the involvement of your company's insurance, legal, and financial professionals. It is important for these "partners" to understand your company and to review your risk management plan and provide feedback. By working as a partner with these advisors, your company's risk management practices become fully integrated into the organization's operations and systems, from the way business is conducted with clients to the way the board operates and the efforts the company makes to maintain its good name in the community.

- *Risk management is holistic.* That means it is hands-on and all-encompassing. Your company's plan addresses risks in a comprehensive and coherent fashion and is reviewed in a regular cycle. The company's insurance broker is a "player," whose advice and input is used to leverage the plan for further benefit to the company. The point of the plan is not to generate "paralysis by analysis," nor does it need to be expensive or labor-intensive. Effective risk management practice strengthens the company and provides the solid framework for maintaining financial and organizational viability for decades to come.

These are examples of the ways genuine risk management practices are implemented in a company. Any business, regardless of its size, can have a solid infrastructure, supported by a board, management, and workforce contingent all of whom are committed to making the company the best it can be.

Linking SOX Best Practices with Your Risk Management Plan

Start by listing all of the SOX best practices and compliance activities that your company has accomplished. This is an important method of

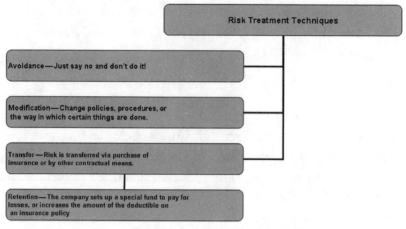

EXHIBIT 8.1   Four Risk Treatment Techniques

demonstrating that your company has implemented sound risk management strategies in each of these areas. For those areas not yet included in SOX best practices, consider how one of these four techniques might be useful in dealing with the risk:

- *Avoidance.* By taking this option you choose to discontinue the activity or practice that appears to be presenting an unacceptably high level of risk. Usually, this option is neither necessary nor desirable.

- *Retention.* This option means that a company can either establish a restricted fund that would be used to address losses from the risk, or significantly raise the deductible on an insurance policy to address the risk (such as automobile policies).

- *Modification.* Modification, the way most risk is generally treated, is the method that considers how the features of a risk can be altered to reduce the potential for frequency or severity of the risk. Typical ways to modify risk include implementing new procedures and protocols, or better training.

- *Transfer.* This option transfers the financial aspects of the risk in a number of ways. The most common is to purchase insurance. Although this option is generally combined with modification, it is by no means an end in itself. Insurance premiums can be raised

EXHIBIT 8 . 2   Risk Management—Basic Steps

significantly by claims; and sometimes, if the number of claims is high, coverage may be canceled or made unavailable. Furthermore, insurance does not cover other significant expenses—for example, if the court should award punitive damages for egregious behavior. If a company receives this type of judgment, it would not be covered by insurance.

These four techniques are illustrated in Exhibit 8.1.

RISK MANAGEMENT ACTIVITIES

Establishing a risk management plan involves three primary risk management activities: assessment, management implementation, and administration and monitoring. Note how these are diagrammed in Exhibit 8.2 before reading the description of each in the following subsections.

Risk Assessment

Risk assessment is the activity that determines which risks the company faces and the potential severity of their impact on the well-being of the business. As you examine each of the operational areas for potential risks in your company, *do not* attempt to make an exhaustive list. Rather, concentrate on those risks that appear to be particularly troublesome, or risk areas that have already caused accidents or injuries, legal problems, or other adverse effects. Because risk management is an ongoing process, those risks that are not addressed this year (or in this round) will be addressed in subsequent rounds.

Here are the steps to developing a risk assessment report:

1. *List the risks that you have identified to this point.* Your list should contain what you consider to be a manageable number of risk issues from each of the four organizational components: management and governance, human resources, operations (be sure to identify risk issues in each of the company's divisions or departments), and public relations.

2. *Decide how you intend to deal with each risk.* Identify which of the techniques for treating risk, given in the previous section, would apply to each risk. Note that sometimes more than one technique will apply; also, it's perfectly acceptable to blend approaches as long as they do not contradict one another or create confusion about how the risk is to be addressed. For any given risk, you can choose to *modify* the conditions that relate to it, you can *transfer* the risk to some extent by purchasing insurance, and you can *retain* part of the risk by having a relatively high insurance deductible. Remember, however, that when you choose a higher deductible, you need to ensure that sufficient funds are always available to cover the deductible in the event of an insured loss. If you choose to *transfer* the risk and purchase insurance, you must also be aware of the conditions of coverage, as well as the exclusions. There are some standard exclusions for property insurance, such as flood, war, and civil unrest. Other types of financial losses are not covered because they are uninsurable such as war.

3. *Assign individuals or groups to carry out the action items.* These action items will comprise the current year's risk management program. Remember, risk management should be part of everyone's

performance expectations, so these items should include risk management activities for every division within the company.

4. *Begin to develop a list of risks to address in the second round.* The risks in the next round (next year) of the risk management process are usually from the initial list drawn up, but not selected to address during the first round. These tiers of risks and the techniques identified for dealing with them will serve as the foundation for developing your risk management program.

Designing a Risk Management Program

The first step in designing a risk management program is to prioritize the risks. Which of the risks that you have identified are the most important, or hazardous, to your company? How many of these risk areas would you be able to realistically address in the next three months? Six months? One year? That's how you should begin to assess the risks. Those that need immediate attention go into the three-month category, and so on.

The risk management program is an interactive document that you will consult regularly and modify and review at specific time intervals. Therefore, you will want to store the program both electronically and in hard copy form in a loose-leaf binder, which is put within easy access. You should also give a copy of the program to everyone on the board and to every employee. Each person should understand that he or she is responsible for helping to monitor the program.

Leveraging Sarbanes-Oxley Best Practices to Build Your Risk Management Plan

Implementation of Sarbanes-Oxley best practices in the areas of IT and electronic document management compliance can serve to strengthen your company's internal controls, raise awareness of cyber-risks throughout the company, produce a higher level of efficiency and productivity, and help to maintain the public trust by securing electronic access to Web sites, databases, and confidential information.

Familiarize yourself with these risk management practices from SOX requirements and best practices:

- Finance
    - Provide accurate financial documents to board and senior management.
    - Document procedures for preparing bank deposits or deposits to other investment houses or other financial institutions and for reconciling the statements from these institutions.
    - Document disbursements and maintain corresponding invoices or receipts for each transaction.
    - Record electronic transactions, particularly sales via the company's Web site.
    - Actively monitor company-owned credit cards, debit cards, and vendor accounts to ensure accuracy and appropriate use.
    - Institute a system for the confidential reporting of waste, fraud, and abuse.
- Information Technology—software, compatibility, storage of electronic documents
    - Ensure privacy and security of sensitive material such as client credit card numbers, Social Security numbers, and other personal information.
    - Designate the person who "owns" your company's Web site. Hint: It shouldn't be the person who designed the site. List your company's authorized Web administrator as the contact on www.whois.com.
    - Install effective firewalls and virus protection.
    - Data storage and security: Make sure your databases and software are able to "communicate" with each other. Allow data access or manipulation to only those individuals you have authorized to do so.
    - In your technology policy, define proper email usage and Internet access.
- Operations (including inventory)
    - Establish security protocols for warehouse and inventory storage.

- Implement privacy protocols to protect confidential client information.
- Implement protocols to track sales and inventory, to prevent pilferage.
- Set policies and procedures to deal with transportation risks.
- Management and governance (if your company has a board)
  - Verify that your board members understand their obligations and heightened level of accountability.
  - Confirm that senior management and the board understand their legal and fiduciary obligations. Put both a conflict of interest policy and code of ethics in place.
  - Have all executive compensation packages approved by the board.
  - Do succession planning for senior management and the board.
- Company image and reputation
  - Handle complaints from neighbors and the community in a sensitive manner.
  - Train your employees to be good citizens when out in the community delivering your goods or driving your vehicles.
  - Commit to excellent customer service. Customer service issues can quickly become image problems if even one customer tells all of his or her associates about the poor-quality service he or she received when dealing with your company.

Developing the Risk Management Plan

The risk assessment and risk management implementation strategies combine to become your company's overall risk management plan. The plan maps out the company's current status in terms of risk, which includes a brief review of the risk management strategies (such as SOX best practices) that are currently in place. Look at Exhibit 8.3, which contains a sample table of contents for the Huxley Pet Shop's risk management plan, to get an idea how to lay out your plan.

Remember to store the plan in an electronic file and/or in hard copy in a large loose-leaf binder, and store back-up copies off-site. Also,

EXHIBIT 8.3   HUXLEY'S PET SHOP RISK
MANAGEMENT PLAN: TABLE
OF CONTENTS

Risk Assessment Report for the Fiscal Year or Calendar year 20XX

Company Profile
The company profile gives the reader information on the size, location, and products
and services that the company provides. The profile also identifies those
SOX requirements and best practices that have already been put into place.

Risk Management Plan
Describes the actions needed to address the risks identified in the risk assessment.

First-priority risks—the risk areas that need to be addressed immediately

- Resources needed to address these risks
- Techniques for each risk
- Responsibilities and time lines
- Desired outcomes/measurements of success
- Documentation of prior claims, occurrences

Second priority risks—the risk areas that should be addressed in the next six to nine
months

- Resources needed to address these risks
- Techniques for each risk
- Responsibilities and time lines
- Desired outcomes/measurements of success
- Documentation of prior claims, occurrences

---

don't forget to schedule a plan review at least twice a year, and outline
steps the company will take to ensure that risk assessment, risk management implementation, and risk administration and monitoring take
place on a regular basis.

Risk Administration and Monitoring

The contents of your company's risk management plan will describe
in detail the actions needed to address the risks identified in the risk
assessment phase. For the purpose of the report, place emphasis on first-
priority risks—those risk areas that need to be addressed immediately.

Be sure to describe how these elements will be blended to craft strategies for treating the identified risks. The strategies need to include:

- *Resources needed to address these risks.* Will the company need to reallocate current resources, either human resources or financial, to administer the risk management plan? If so, identify exactly what will be necessary to implement an effective strategy. It may simply be a policy change or greater commitment to enforcement. The point is, don't automatically "throw money" at the problem unless you can demonstrate that the expenditures are essential to bring about the desire outcome.

- *Techniques for each risk.* Describe the technique that you will use to treat each identified risk. Modification is the one most often used to bring about lasting change.

- *Responsibilities and time lines.* It is essential that you assign responsibility and accountability appropriately, identify deliverables, and establish time lines for results.

- *Desired outcomes/measurements of success.* To evaluate whether your risk management strategies are successful, you need to establish *simple metrics*—for example, setting an X percent reduction in worker's compensation claims.

- *Documentation of prior claims and risk issues.* Reviewing a recent history (three years) of insurance claims or risk issues can be particularly useful in identifying those factors that contribute to accidents and other adverse occurrences.

Once you've addressed your first-priority risks, you'll need to decide on the strategies you plan to use to deal with second-priority risks and schedule timing for taking action. Consider the following components:

- Resources needed to address these risks
- Techniques for each risk
- Responsibilities and time lines
- Desired outcomes/measurements of success
- Documentation of prior claims, risk issues

Setting Dates for the Next Round of Risk Management Planning

Be sure to set a date for the next round of risk management planning, preferably three to six months from the writing of the report on first-priority risk management. Your goal is to make risk management planning and best practices a routine part of the company's operations. Routine review and modification are essential to the successful integration of risk management within every department of the company.

Administration and Monitoring of Risk Management Decisions

You will begin administering and monitoring your risk management plan as soon as the decisions have been made on how to treat the current list of risk areas. Your objective is twofold: 1) to make sure the risk treatment strategy is actually working and 2) to ensure that the actions taken in the risk management implementation stage are reviewed to determine effectiveness as well as to establish a framework for the next round of risk assessment. You might find the strategies worked as anticipated, or they did not. Keep in mind that unforeseen consequences are always a possibility. If a strategy doesn't work as expected, chalk it up to experience and be prepared to try another approach.

There are a number of ways to evaluate the success of the risk management strategies that you applied to specific risks. Here are some good questions to ask:

- *Did the number of accidents decrease?* Documentation is always important, but even more so once a risk management program is in place.

- *Were any accidents/problems documented and analyzed?* It's important to document not only actual risk occurrences, but also the "near misses." There may be a pattern that has not yet come to light.

- *What about insurance claims—frequency and severity of losses?* Insurance claims are filed because a loss occurred that was covered by the policy. All insurance claims need to be documented. Your insurance professional can provide copies of claims if your files need to be updated. Once the risk management plan is in place, your company will want to track the number of claims that are filed to determine if the number of claims has decreased, and by what percent.

- *How many employee complaints were filed?* If, for example, the company's risk management strategies have raised a "hot button" issue in terms of employee morale, it is important to track the number of complaints that come in after the risk treatment has been executed.

- *Were internal control policies and procedures put in place and adequately enforced?* Two of the major areas of change, whether to achieve SOX compliance or carry out risk management planning, are the company's internal controls system and the implementation of policies and procedures. An important goal of risk management activities, and SOX compliance, is the strengthening of the company's internal controls and infrastructure. Successful implementation of these new policies and procedures is possible only if they are enforced. Changes in behavior and expectations are key elements in introducing effective risk management. Consider this aspect of risk management planning as another opportunity to stress compliance to your employees.

BUSINESS CONTINUITY PLANNING

The tragedy of September 11, 2001, illustrated two important lessons about business continuity planning. Morgan Stanley was one of the companies that had offices in the World Trade Center. This firm was well aware of the damage a terrorist attack could cause, having been one of the victims of the previous terrorist bombing at the World Trade Center, in 1993, which inflicted heavy damage on the Morgan Stanley offices. Thus, Morgan Stanley's managers understood that it was not a case of if, but when the next attack took place. So following the 1993 bombing, Morgan Stanley brought in a consultant to put its staff through monthly disaster drills. The expectation was that during these drills, everyone was to exit the building via the nearest emergency exit. These drills took place every month for the next eight years.

Luckily for the Morgan Stanley employees, their offices were located on the lower floors of the World Trade Center, so when the alarm sounded on September 11, 2001, everyone in the Morgan Stanley offices evacuated the building and kept moving. Very few members of the Morgan Stanley staff lost their lives that morning.

Two important lessons from September 11 are:

1. Business interruptions are a "part of life" at any company and should be expected to occur. Of course, few business interruption are caused by terrorist activities, but any type interruption can send the company's operations into crisis mode.

2. Business interruptions need not destroy the company, if a plan is in place to manage crisis incidents and resume business operations.

Would your company be able to survive a crisis that interrupted business operations?

What Is Business Continuity Planning?

▓ It is 8:00 P.M. on a Saturday night. A fire has started in the building housing the Huxley Pet Shop. By the time the firefighters arrive, the entire shop is engulfed. Sprinklers throughout the building have been activated and there is approximately three feet of standing water on each floor. The building has been "red-tagged," as the firefighters have determined that the flooring in the shop has been seriously compromised, and in several places the floor has crashed down to the basement below. Wiring and telecommunications infrastructure also have been seriously damaged. Building inspectors believe that the building will remain red-tagged for at least six weeks. ▓

If you were the owner of the Huxley Pet Shop would you know what to do? How would you notify your business partners and your

EXHIBIT 8.4   CRISIS COMMUNICATION PLAN WORKSHEET

Does your company's crisis communication plan have these components?
Communication and media relations plan
- A designated spokesperson and a back-up spokesperson who are trained in communications and media relations.
  - Important! All staff and volunteers should understand that *all* media inquiries are to be directed to the designated spokesperson. This is to ensure that all information given to the media is accurate and up to date. Employees need to know that there are severe penalties for breaching this protocol.
- A prepared statement that can be used in the event of a crisis. The statement is prepared in advance and has these talking points:
  - Basic facts—name of the company, location, and brief description of the company's mission.
  - A section (to be filled in when a crisis occurs) that describes the following (details until facts and circumstances can be verified):
    - What happened, in very general terms
    - Who was involved
    - When the crisis occurred
    - Where the crisis occurred
  - Information on how to contact the company
  - The company's commitment to the community and its customers

Supporting employees, customers, and other stakeholders
- In the event of a crisis, employees need to know how to obtain information on the situation and what is expected of them in terms of service.
- Clients will need to know how to contact the company either to obtain goods and services or to contact alternative resources.

---

employees, so that they all know what to do/where to go on Monday morning?

Business continuity planning (BCP) is the process a company uses to develop and document the policies, procedures, activities, and protocols they deem necessary to resume essential business operations immediately following a business interruption. Based on this definition, it's clear that BCP is an important companion piece to risk management planning. A well-crafted risk management plan can facilitate the design of an effective business continuity plan and, conversely, a well-crafted business continuity plan can be the foundation for the design of a risk management plan.

There are three primary components to a business continuity plan:

1. *Crisis incident management component.* The initial crisis scenario must be addressed before the company can even consider the steps it needs to take to resume operation. In today's media-driven environment, a solid crisis communications strategy is essential to preserving your company's good name and providing quality information to support emergency customer service. Exhibit 8.4 gives you a worksheet for developing a communication plan to use following a business interruption.

2. *Business resumption component.* Once the company has dealt with the immediate crisis, it needs to begin work immediately to resume operations. This stage of the plan should clearly describe the company's important functions and prioritize/sequence the functional areas that must be in place to resume operations.

3. *Emergency customer service component.* The emergency customer service component often occurs in parallel with the crisis incident management and the business resumption components. Your customers need to know how to reach you and how their dealings with your company will be affected, and for how long, by the interruption.

What Are the Causes of Business Interruptions?

Interruptions to the normal flow of operations at your company can have any number of causes. Those caused by nature, such as earthquakes, are very difficult to predict—although you may receive some advance notice of others, such as hurricanes, tornadoes, and floods. Civil actions, such as riots, police activity, or large-scale demonstrations, also typically unpredictable, can also disrupt your company's operations. Even a major traffic jam, street closure due to an accident, or rupture of a sewer or gas main without warning can interfere with the daily life of your business. But some of the most disruptive and long-lasting interruptions are caused by humans with bad intentions. Computer hackers, who launch computer viruses or "worm" infestations, have the potential for doing irreparable damage to databases and hard drives. And, sadly, workplace violence, including bomb threats, has become a more common cause of interruption. The result of this type of interruption can be devastating for the company.

Your company may also find it necessary to redirect some of its resources in the wake of a loss of a major client or a contract. Many companies do not always recognize this type of an event as a business interruption, but it is. The loss of a significant income stream and/or the potential to secure the renewal of a major contract can signal the need to curtail important programs and/or to address a loss of reputation in the community.

An interruption in operations may also be the result of the loss of essential members of the staff or executive team. This type of interruption would become particularly acute if the individual(s) possessed knowledge, networking connections, or institutional history that either was not documented or shared with individuals in the company.

Designing the Plan

Like any important operational planning, for it to be effective, business continuity planning must have absolute commitment by the board and senior management. These individuals need to clearly endorse the need for the plan and articulate the expectation for completion of the plan within the time frame specified. Further, those individuals assigned to lead the project need to introduce and explain BCP concepts to all employee and managers. This process can be streamlined by the creation of a cross-functional team, whose members need to be privy to all of the SOX best practices that have been put in place at your company.

The BCP planning team's agenda should:

- *Identify possible business interruptions.* This exercise should *briefly* consider both likely as well as less likely interruptions. The deliverable from this exercise should be an overview of the possible interruptions, ranked in terms of severity. Again, don't spend a lot of time on this discussion. Remember, there are myriad causes of interruptions.

- *Determine crucial functions.* To establish strategies for business resumption, it is important to determine which operational activities and functions are essential for your company to continue doing business. Who performs these activities and functions? Are there written protocols and procedures outlining these activities and functions? What would happen if the person who usually does an essential function were not available? Who would take that person's place? Some examples of essential functions include:
  - *Administration, human resources, and payroll.* These are three important areas of the organization's infrastructure. In the event of a natural disaster, many people find that they no longer have jobs. Your company needs to establish strategies to assure your employees that they will have jobs, but they also need to be informed of their own obligations to the company, such as agreeing to work in shifts or serve in a different functional area, as necessary, until things return to normal.
  - *Finance.* The finance function includes procedures related to the company's general operating funds, insurance coverage, claims procedures, and loss documentation. Additionally, your company will need to consider how to use credit sources for business resumption. Check writing and monitoring, as well as fund transferring and wiring, are means of financing expenses related to mitigation steps. Security procedures related to confidential transactions and other codes also need to be in place.
  - *Customer service.* The BCP needs to include a clear description of the menu of services provided to your company's clients. In the event of an interruption, it is possible that this list will have to be revised to include only the priority services.
  - *Information technology.* Your company's IT systems are essential to resuming operations following an interruption. The sooner your company can access its email, electronic files, and electronic databases, the faster you will be back in full operation.
  - *Sales and inventory.* Your company will need to determine how it plans to fulfill customer orders if the business interruption either destroys inventory or prevents the company from accessing the inventory to ship it.

- *Other important business functions.* The plan needs to address all of the company's essential business functions, meaning those that would have to be in place and operational before the company could resume business.

Typical Plan Protocols

The next step has two parts: (1) to set up procedures to deal with the immediate emergency, and (2) to institute the procedures for resuming operations. For example, a procedure to deal with an immediate emergency would include how to evacuate employees, clients, and visitors from the building. The BCP should have a section that describes in detail evacuation procedures, emergency exits, and the like.

Crisis communication planning is essential to any business continuity plan. The following components should be included in your company's business continuity plan:

- Communication with stakeholders such as board members, employees, and customers will be important to provide necessary information and to appeal for assistance.

- Public relations and media contacts will be important for disseminating information about the emergency to the community, and to explain how the public can help.

- Other important aspects of the plan are alternative work and service delivery sites, including employee status, availability, and notification.

Once your company has incorporated SOX best practices, composing the BCP becomes easier and faster. Here are a number of elements of the BCP that are facilitated by incorporating SOX best practices:

- *Financial procedures and methods for storing and archiving financial documents.* By adopting SOX best practices, your company already has procedures in place for document storage and back-up. Likewise, financial procedures are in place and internal controls have been strengthened.

- *Senior management roles and expectations.* The SOX best practices your company has implemented will help your board members to have a better understanding of their roles in the company's operation, in particular in the event of an emergency.

- *Document retention system, to include remote access to data files.* The SOX legislation requires that your company establish document retention policies and procedures.

- *Identification of resource needs for business resumption and location of these resources.* As your company adopts the SOX best practices, particularly as these relate to the annual audit, the company will need to review its current vendor and service provider list to ensure that all contracts and arrangements are in order.

Keeping the Plan Viable

Like the risk management plan, the BCP has to be reviewed and revised on a regular basis to keep it viable. With any contingency plan, it is advisable to stage a crisis simulation to determine, for example, how fast employees can exit the building or how well a phone tree works.

In sum, your company benefits from having both a risk management and a business continuity plan, because each has a specific focus to ensure that the firm's internal controls and processes stay on track and that new risks or issues are addressed in routine reviews.

HOW PROFESSIONAL EXPERTS CAN HELP YOU FACILITATE SOX COMPLIANCE AND BEST PRACTICES

Depending on the size of your company, you may work with any number of outside professional experts, among them:

- Legal counsel

- Insurance professional

- Financial professionals—bankers, investment counselors, accountants, and auditors

- IT specialist
- Payroll vendor

These individuals bring very specific types of expertise to the table, for which your company pays handsomely. In your company's efforts to implement SOX requirements and best practices and to develop risk management or business continuity planning, don't overlook the benefits of building and maintaining solid working relationships with these professionals; they can provide your company with indispensable advice.

- They know and understand your company and its operations. This institutional knowledge is crucial in tailoring the implementation of SOX requirements and best practices. They also know what you might already have in place and can help you to avoid duplicated efforts, which waste time and money.
- Professionals have access to the latest information and research. If your company's operational profile is unusual, these experts can work with you to develop SOX implementation and risk management or business continuity approaches that work for you.
- Professionals can assist you in framing your SOX compliance and risk or business continuity profile and provide important guidance. The company profile can be a highly useful tool in gaining access to insurance markets, improving your credit rating, and improving your company's competitive positioning.

Legal Counsel

Your company's attorney provides essential advice and review of documents, guides decisions, and offers advice on legal situations that could present problems for your business. Additionally, your attorney can help your company remain in compliance with laws and regulations, as he or she has ready access to current findings and legal decisions.

Generally, attorneys bill by the hour, but in today's competitive environment, some are willing to contract with clients in "project" mode. If your company is about to begin implementation of SOX requirements and best practices, you might want to ask whether your attorney would be willing to provide assistance on a package basis. This is particularly important if your company needs to draft the following types of documents:

- Whistleblower protection policy
- Prohibition against destruction of documents policy
- Code of ethics
- Conflict of interest policy

As noted repeatedly throughout this manuscript, you should always have your attorney review the wording and tone of all your policies, to ensure that the spirit of the documents is appropriately conveyed and that they are crafted correctly to address the issues at hand.

Insurance Professional

Your company's insurance professional is a very valuable resource not only for reviewing your risk management and business continuity planning, but also for your SOX implementation. He or she can help you to craft your company's risk profile so that underwriters will have no trouble recognizing your efforts to come into compliance and adapt best practices. Your company's insurance professional also can help you to craft a risk management plan that illustrates your company's commitment to being a full partner in managing risks and keeping down the cost of insurance.

Another important aspect of this relationship focuses on facilitating a higher level of understanding in terms of what factors affect the availability of insurance, premium costs, and your company's access to the insurance industry. This person assists your company in addressing the factors used by the industry to evaluate potential insureds, which include:

- *Finances.* Your company's financial condition can either earn confidence or raise suspicion. The SOX best practice of having reliable financial statements becomes very important as insurance underwriters evaluate your company for potential coverage.

- *Scope and nature of operations.* What your company does or produces can create a heightened exposure. Having risk management and business continuity plans that clearly demonstrate SOX compliance will be helpful in establishing underwriter confidence.
- *Affiliates, subsidiaries, and the risks posed by these entities.* Your company may be a preferred vendor to a larger company who was just accused of fraudulent billing practices. Would the affiliation with this company create liability for your company?
- *Location(s) of operations.* Is your company located on Three Mile Island or in a pristine wilderness location? Factors in the community or external environment can affect insurance coverage and premiums.
- *Loss history (and mitigation activities).* Your company should prepare an extensive history of insurance claims to present to the underwriter. At the same time, your company should be prepared to provide proof that mitigation activities are taking place, ideally in the form of an ongoing risk management program.
- *Workplace safety and worker's compensation experience.* Workplace safety and worker's compensation claims are consistently among the top three reasons for insurance claims and litigation in companies. The other two reasons are wrongful termination and sexual harassment. Clearly, your company's track record in workplace safety issues will be an essential aspect of the underwriter's review.
- *Risk management expertise.* Having risk management and business continuity plans in place will provide solid evidence of your company's expertise in these areas.
- *Relationships with mortgagees, lenders, third parties, and others.* The underwriter may want to know what type of risk these stakeholders view your company as presenting. Having good relationships with these stakeholders offers benefits in a number of areas.

If your insurance professional isn't someone who is particularly close to the firm, consider finding one who is willing to be, so that your company can secure and maintain the best coverage possible at the best price.

Financial Professionals

Your company has several financial professionals working in distinct areas. These professionals include your:

- Auditor, whose only job should be to conduct an audit for your firm.

- Tax consultant, who prepares your company's annual tax returns.

- Payroll vendor, who produces and distributes your company's payroll. This is an important financial professional, particularly if your company outsources this function to a nationally recognized firm.

- Banker, who not only acts as a liaison between your company and the bank, but is a resource for ways your banking transactions can be made more secure.

As your company begins its work to bring the firm into compliance with SOX requirements and best practices, it is essential that you consult with these experts to fashion your company's Blueprint activities. Your auditor is particularly important, as he or she might produce a management letter in which specific areas that need immediate attention are identified. If you receive such a document, deal with these issues immediately! Be sure to document your actions and be prepared to show proof that the problems were remedied. There is no substitute for having a clean audit!

Financial professionals need to know your company inside and out. If they don't, arrange to inform them on your firm and arrange for routine follow-ups. These professionals can also identify other services that their firms can provide that will streamline your processes and create the types of reports and data analyses that you might need for filings or other scheduled reporting. If you outsource your payroll with a nationally recognized firm or with a large bank, these vendors could offer specific products besides payroll services tailored to meet the needs of your firm. If you are inclined to say, "No thanks, I can do it for free in-house," think again. *Nothing done "in-house" is free.* Further, these vendors have a level of expertise that automatically generates an efficiency of scale.

Your tax consultant and banker can provide excellent guidance as your company begins work on SOX best practices, particularly internal controls related to finance. Have these individuals review your current internal controls and provide feedback.

IT Specialist

Your company's IT specialist is a professional in his or her own right. Some business owners might fail to recognize this because IT specialists rarely don suits and ties to call on clients. Nevertheless, this professional is one of your company's key resources in coming into compliance with SOX, implementing SOX best practices, as well as establishing and maintaining effective risk management and business continuity plans.

Discuss in detail your plans to implement SOX requirements and best practices with your company's IT specialist so that he or she can tailor the next steps, to address your company's growth potential and its need for other plans such as risk management and business continuity. Your current IT system has to be configured so that it is consistent with SOX expectations, as one day your company may want to launch an IPO. At that point, your IT system must be in compliance with all of the stipulations in SOX section 404, or whichever administrative rules are written over the years.

As your business grows, it becomes increasingly important to enable your company's IT system to grow with it, at the same time it addresses the firm's relevant legal requirements. If your company outsources its IT function, this creates a vulnerability in the event of a community-wide disaster. Consider the small businesses in New Orleans affected by Hurricane Katrina. Even if these businesses were able to reopen in a relatively short time frame, they might not have been able to either locate or access their IT specialists. Discuss these concerns frankly with your IT specialist and, if necessary, begin to build a relationship with a back-up vendor.

MAXIMIZING THE VALUE OF YOUR RELATIONSHIPS WITH PROFESSIONALS

Your company pays its professional experts well to provide important services. It is important that you as the small business owner learn to leverage your current relationships with these experts to ensure that you obtain the quality of information you need to streamline your implementation of SOX requirements and best practices. For that reason, as stated earlier, be sure that each of these professionals has thorough knowledge of your company's operations and infrastructure. Don't hesitate to call on these experts for advice. Even if you are billed by the hour, consider it money well spent. Making costly errors because you didn't want to spend the money to obtain expert advice is irresponsible. Your company, its investors, employees, customers, and stakeholders deserve better.

Consider what you can do to improve these professional experts' understanding of your company and its unique needs. Similarly, consider how you might become a full partner with each one of them to improve the quality and effectiveness of the relationship. If you are not sure of how you might become a better collaborator, ask!

Red Flags

At the same time you are working to develop your relationships with professional advisors, you need to be on the lookout for signs that you might not have a good match with one or more of them. Don't ignore these red flags:

- The professional does not return your calls in a timely manner.
- You can't get answers that make sense, just lots of jargon, but nothing that you really understand.
- The professional is unwilling to present his or her marketing strategy for your company to another decision maker, such as an insurance company.
- The professional is not interested in working with you to develop action strategies for SOX requirements, best practices, or risk management and business continuity plans.

- The professional insists that the current offering of products or services is the best he or she can provide. You know you need something else, but the person is unwilling to work with you to find a customized solution.

- The professional is paid on commission and is reluctant to disclose the commission percentage—or even to disclose whether he or she is salaried or on commission. You as a consumer have a right to know this, and if the person charges by the hour, you have a right to know the hourly fee and any other charges that might be applicable.

- The professional does anything else that suggests a lack of integrity or makes you suspicious, uncomfortable, or reluctant to work with the person.

If any of these red flags apply to any of the professionals you work with, begin to look for a replacement immediately. Contact professional organizations, local chambers of commerce, and even trusted business associates to help you find a replacement. Trust your instincts, if you sense something wrong! There are many, many excellent professionals from which to choose. Don't settle for second best or be made to feel like you have to settle for inferior quality because you are a small businessperson.

NEXT STEPS

It's time to begin the process of complying with SOX requirements and best practices. It is important to remember that any system or process that doesn't make sense won't be used. Tailoring SOX compliance, best practices, risk management, and business continuity planning to the specific needs and profile of your company is a must. There is no other company out there like yours, so make sure that the policies and procedures are logical and user-friendly. Best wishes for much success!

Bibliography

Abernathy, K.Q. (2002). "Special Alert: What WorldCom Bankruptcy Means to Consumers," Focus on Consumer Concerns, vol. 2(5). Retrieved on August 15, 2004, from www.fcc .gov/commissioners/abernathy/news/worldcom.html.

About the Great Depression. (n.d.). Retrieved on September 24, 2004, from www.english .uiuc.edu/maps/depression/about.htm.

AICPA. (n.d.). Sarbanes-Oxley Act/PCAOB Implementation Central. Retrieved on June 25, 2004, from www.aicpa.org/sarbanes/index.asp.

————. (2005). "Summary of Sarbanes-Oxley Act of 2002." American Institute of Certified Public Accountants. Retrieved on April 2, 2005, from www.aicpa.org/info/sarbanes_oxley _summary.htm.

AllBusiness.Com: The Advisor. (June 1, 2005). "Know the Difference Between Regular and Contract Workers." San Francisco, CA: SF Gate.

Anthony, Joseph. (2005). "Private Companies: 4 Lessons from Sarbanes-Oxley Act." Microsoft Small Business Center. Retrieved on July 21, 2005, from www.microsoft.com/smallbusiness/ resources/finance/legal_expenses/private_companies_4_lessons.

Arthur Andersen LLP v. United States. No. 04–368. (2005). Retrieved on July 21, 2005, from http://caselaw.lp.findlaw.com/scripts/getcase.pl?court=US&vol=000&invol=04–368&friend= usatoday#opinion1.

Association of Certified Fraud Examiners. (1996). "Report to the Nation." Retrieved on July 1, 2005, from www.cfenet.com/pdfs/Report_to_the_Nation.pdf.

Bahls, Steven C., and Jane Easter Bahls. (May 2003). "Criminal Records," Entrepreneur Magazine, http://www.entrepreneur.com/.

Beasley, Mark S., Joseph Carcello, Dana R. Hermanson, and Paul D. Lapides. (December 2000). "Fraudulent Financial Reporting: Consideration of Industry Traits and Corporate Governance Mechanisms," Accounting Horizons, vol. 14, no. 4, December 2000, pp. 441–454.

Beasley, Mark S., Joseph Carcello, and Dana R. Hermanson. (April 2001). "Top 10 Audit Deficiencies," Journal of Accountancy, vol. 191, no. 4, http://www.aicpa.org/PUBS/jofa/ apr2001/beasley.htm.

Beattie, A. (2003). Why It's All Our Fault: How Investors Often Cause the Market's Problems. Retrieved on June 17, 2004, from www.investopedia.com/articles/basics/03/062003.asp.

Beltran, L. (2002). "Waksal Indicted in ImClone Scandal." CNN/Money. Retrieved on March 16, 2005, from http://money.cnn.com/2002/08/07/news/waksal_indictment/.

Bonello, F. J. (2004). Stock Exchange. Microsoft Encarta Online Encyclopedia. Retrieved on May 23, 2004, from http://encarta.msn.com/encyclopedia_761560145_2/Stock_Exchange .html#p67.

Broude, Paul D., and Richard L. Prebil. (March 2005). The Impact of Sarbanes-Oxley on Private and Nonprofit Companies. Chicago, IL: Foley & Lardner LLP.

Bumgardner, L.J. (2003). "How Does the Sarbanes-Oxley Act Impact American Business?" Journal of Contemporary Business Practice, vol. 6(1). Retrieved on July 19, 2004, from http://gbr.pepperdine.edu/031/sarbanesoxley.html.

Carpenter, Tina D., M.B. Fennema, Phillip Z. Fretwell, and William Hillison. (March 2004). "A Changing Corporate Culture," Journal of Accountancy, vol. 197, no. 3, http://www.aicpa .org/PUBS/JOFA/mar2004/carpent.htm.

CNN.com (1998). "The Market 'Circuit Breakers': How They Work." Retrieved on July 17, 2004, from www.cnn.com/US/9809/01/market.circuit.breakers/.

Cohen, Jay. (May 2004). "Protecting Privacy in an Exposed Business Environment." IDA/Kahn Conference Proceedings, San Jose, CA.

Corporate and Auditing Accountability, Responsibility, and Transparency Act of 2002, H.R. 3763, 107th Congress. Retrieved on January 28, 2004, from http://thomas.loc.gov/cgi-bin/ query/D?c107:1:./temp/~c107GaX96X.

COSO (1999). Fraudulent Financial Reporting: 1987(1997: An Analysis of U.S. Public Companies–Executive Summary and Introduction. Retrieved on April 29, 2005, from www.coso.org/publications/executive_summary_fraudulent_financial_reporting.htm.

———. (1992). Internal Control–Integrated Framework: Executive Summary. Retrieved on April 29, 2005, from www.coso.org/publications/executive_summary_integrated_framework.htm.

———. (1987). Report of the National Commission of Fraudulent Financial Reporting. Retrieved on April 29, 2005, from www.coso.org/publications/NCFFR_Part_1.htm.

Cozad, Matthew A. (October 2005). "Top 5 SOX Best Strategies for Small Companies," Strategic Finance, vol. 87, no. 4, http://www.imanet.org/ima/sec.asp?TRACKID=& CID=1569& DID=3361.

CSBC (2002). "Executive Summary of the Sarbanes-Oxley Act of 2002: P.L. 107–204." Conference of State Bank Supervisors. Retrieved on January 3, 2005, from www.csbs.org/government/legislative/misc/2002_sarbanes-oxley_summary.htm.

Davis, Linda J. (May 2005). "Compliance Programs in 2005: What Is Good Enough?" IDC/Kahn Conference Proceedings, San Jose, CA.

Davis, R.R. (April 2004). "Using Disclaimers in Audit Reports: Discerning between Shades of Opinion," CPA Journal, Online. Retrieved on August 3, 2004, from www.nysscpa.org/cpajournal/2004/404/essentials/p26.htm.

DeBare, Ilana. (June 1, 2005). "Determining Whether Worker Is a Contractor or an Employee. San Francisco, CA: SF Gate.

Doyle, Stephanie. (August 2005). "Grappling with Section 404," International Auditor, vol. 62, no. 4, http://www.findarticles.com/p/articles/mi_m4153/is_4_62/ai_n15890724/print.

Eichenwald, Kurt. (June 15, 2002). "Arthur Andersen Convicted of Obstruction of Justice," New York Times, http://www.nytimes.com.

Fabrizius, Michael P., and Richard M. Sarafini. (February 2004). "Learning to Love the Scrutiny: Initiating a Quality Assessment Can Help an Internal Audit Group Come Out on Top," Internal Auditor, vol. 61, no. 1, p. 38.

Farrell, G. (May 21, 2002). "Anderson Staffer Says Phrase Was a Hint to Shred," USA Today, http://www.usatoday.com.

Fram, Eugene H., and H.J. Zoffer. (2005). "Are American Corporate Directors Still Ignoring the Signals?," Corporate Governance, vol. 5, no 1, http://www.ingentaconnect.com/content/mcb/268/2005/00000005/00000001/art00003.

Gallegos, Frederick, CISA, CGFM, CDE. (2003). Sarbanes-Oxley Act of 2002 and Impact on the IT Auditor. NY, NY: Auerbach Publications.

Gately. E. (2005). "Some Say New SEC Regulations Waste Company Time and Money," East Valley Tribune.com. Retrieved on July 9, 2005, from www.eastvalleytribune.com/index.php?sty=44045.

Gordon, Jeffrey N. (2003). "Governance Failures of the Enron Board and the New Information Order of Sarbanes-Oxley." Columbia Law School Center for Law and Economic Studies, Working Paper, no. 216.

Gullapalli, Diya. (October 17, 2005). "Living with Sarbanes-Oxley," Wall Street Journal, http://www.wsj.com.

Ha, Michael. (September 8, 2003). "Going Private? Keep D&O Cover," National Underwriter, vol. 107, no. 36, http://cms.nationalunderwriter.com/cms/nationalunderwriter/public%20website.

Harrington, Cynthia. (September 2005). "The Value Proposition," Journal of Accountancy, http://www.aicpa.org/PUBS/JOFA/joaiss.htm.

Hermanson, Dana. (July/August 2005). "Is the Sarbanes-Oxley Act Worth It?," Internal Auditing, vol. 20, no 4, http://oversightsystems.com/news_events/InternalAuditing_0508.pdf.

IRS.gov. (June 2002). "The Internal Auditor," Professional Guidance." vol. 59, no. 3.

IRS.gov. (2004). Ann. 2002–87,37.

———(2004). Publication 463: "Travel, Entertainment, Gift and Car Expenses."

IRS.gov. (1999). Bulletin 1999–17: "Internal Revenue Bulletin." Retrieved April 28, 2005, from www.irs.gov/pub/irs-irbs/irb99–17.pdf.

Jackson, Peggy M., and Toni E. Fogarty. (2005). Sarbanes-Oxley for Nonprofits. Hoboken, NJ: John Wiley & Sons, Inc.

———. (2006). Sarbanes-Oxley for Nonprofit Management. Hoboken, NJ: John Wiley & Sons, Inc.

Jackson, Russell A. (August 2005). "There Is No Shortcut to Good Controls," Internal Auditor, vol. 62, no. 4, http://www.findarticles.com/p/articles/mi_m4153/is_4_62/ai_n15890725.

Jacoby, Mary. (October 17, 2005). "Wherever Investors Go, Demands for Better Governance Follow," Wall Street Journal, http://www.wsj.com.

Jefferson Wells, a Manpower Company. (August 2005). "The Changing Sarbanes-Oxley Environment for Small and Medium-Sized Companies: Steps to Take Now."

Johnson, Carrie. (September 22, 2005). "Small Firms Get More Time on Sarbanes-Oxley Rules," Washington Post, http://www.washingtonpost.com.

Kastl, Melanie A., Louis Avitablile, and Brian H. Kleiner. (January/February 2005). "How to Assess Credibility in Workplace Investigations," Nonprofit World, vol. 23(1), http://www.snpo.org/publications/nonprofitworld.php.

Kissi, Dawn. (May 2, 2005). "A Most Painful Act: Enacted to Restore Investor Confidence, Sarbanes-Oxley Is Proving a Costly Fix," Daily News Record, http://www.findarticles.com/p/articles/mi_hb4298/is_200505/ai_n14951924.

Kohn, S.M. (2004). "The Sarbanes-Oxley Act Legal Protections for Corporate Whistleblowers." National Whistleblower Center. Retrieved on February 17, 2005, from http://jobsearchtech.about.com/gi/dynamic/offsite.htm?zi=1/XJ&sdn=jobsearchtech&zu=http%3A%2F%2Fwww.whistleblowers.org%2F.

Kosinski, Gregory, and Jay M. Cohen. (May 2004). "Fundamentals of Compliance," IDA/Kahn Conference Proceedings, San Jose, CA.

Kovach, Lisa. (May 23, 2005). "SBA Tries to Rewrite the Small Biz Definition," San Diego Business Journal, http://www.sdbj.com/.

Lange, Michele, C.S. (April 2003). "Keeping Your Head: New Sarbanes-Oxley Rules Make Document Retention Dizzying," Corporate Counsel Magazine, http://www.law.com/jsp/cc/index.jsp.

Leech, Tim J. (April 2003). "SOX—Sections 302 and 404," white paper, Ontario, Canada.

Lenz, R.T., and J.L. Engledow. (1986). "Environmental Analysis Units and Strategic Decision-Making: A Field Study of Selected 'Leading Edge' Corporations," Strategic Management Journal 7(1), pp. 69–89.

Lieberman, Larry D. (June 2004). "Sarbanes-Oxley Affects Your Private Company Clients," Wisconsin Lawyer, vol. 77, no. 6, http://www.wisbar.org/AM/Template.cfm?Section=Current_Issue1&Template=/WisconsinLawyer.cfm.

Lindbloom, E.E. (1969). "The Sciences of 'Muddling Through.'" In Readings in Modern Organizations, A. Etzioni, ed. Englewood Cliffs, NJ: Prentice Hall.

Mintzberg, H. (1983). Structure in Fives: Designing Effective Organizations. Englewood Cliffs, NJ: Prentice Hall.

Moore, Geoffrey. (March 2003). "Managing Electronic Records Is No Longer Optional. White paper, published by Information Managers, Edison, NJ.

Office of the Press Secretary of the President of the United States. (2002). "Executive Order Establishment of the Corporate Fraud Task Force." Retrieved on February 17, 2005, from www.whitehouse.gov/news/releases/2002/07/20020709–2.html.

————. (2002). "President Bush Signs Corporate Corruption Bill." Retrieved on February 21, 2005, from www.whitehouse.gov/news/releases/2002/07/20020730.html.

Patsuris, P. (2002). "The Corporate Scandal Sheet." Retrieved on June 2, 2005, from www.forbes.com/2002/07/25/accountingtracker.html.

Payroll Manager's Letter. (March 7, 2005). "Employee or Independent Contractor? Points to Consider in Worker Classification." Aspen Publishers, Inc., vol. 21, no. 5.

Perry, Phillip M. (September-October 2004). "Employee or Independent Contractor? The IRS Wants to Know," Rural Telecommunications, National Telephone Cooperative Association, vol. 21, no. 5.

Public Company Accounting Oversight Board. (2003). "Accounting Support Fees." Retrieved on June 17, 2005, from www.pcaobus.org/Support_Fees/index.asp.

————. (2003). "About PCAOB." Retrieved on June 17, 2005, from www.pcaobus.org/About_Us/index.asp.

————. (2005). "Board Revokes Firm's Registration, Disciplines Three Accountants for Failure to Cooperate," Public Affairs 202–207–9227. Retrieved on June 7, 2005, from www.pcaobus.org/News_and_Events/News/2005/05–24.asp.

———. (2005). "Bylaws and Rules of the Public Company Accounting Oversight Board." Retrieved on June 17, 2005, from www.pcaobus.org/Rules_of_the_Board/Documents/Rules_of _the_Board/all.pdf.

———. (2003). "Frequently Asked Questions Regarding Registration with the Board." PCAOB Release 2003–011A. Retrieved on June 17, 2005, from www.pcaobus.org/Rules_of_the _Board/Documents/Release2003–011A.pdf.

———. (2005). "Frequently Asked Questions: The Accounting Support Fee and the Funding Process." Retrieved on June 20, 2005, from www.pcaob.org/Support_Fees/SupportFeeFAQ .pdf.

———. (2005). "Order Instituting Disciplinary Proceedings, Making Findings and Imposing Sanctions in the Matter of Alan J. Goldberger, CPA, and William A. Postelnick, CPA." PCAOB Release No. 2005–011. Retrieved on June 18, 2005, from www.pcaobus.org/ Enforcement/Disciplinary_Proceedings/2005/05–24_Goldberger_and_Postelnik.pdf.

———. (2005). "Order Instituting Disciplinary Proceedings, Making Findings and Imposing Sanctions in the Matter of Goldstein and Morris, CPAs, P.C., and Edward B. Morris, CPA." PCAOB Release No. 2005–010. Retrieved on June 18, 2005, from www.pcaobus.org/ Enforcement/Disciplinary_Proceedings/2005/05–24_Goldstein_and_Morris.pdf.

———. (2003). "PCAOB Center for Enforcement Tips, Complaints, and Other Information." Retrieved on June 17, 2005, from www.pcaobus.org/Enforcement/Tips/index.asp.

———. (2004). "PCAOB 2004 Budget." Retrieved on June 17, 2005, from www.pcaobus.org/ About_Us/Budget_Presentations/2004.pdf.

———. (2005). "PCAOB 2005 Budget (Revised)." Retrieved on June 17, 2005, from www .pcaobus.org/About_Us/Budget_Presentations/2005.pdf.

———. (2004). "Statement Concerning the Issuance of Inspection Reports." PCAOB Release No. 104–2004–001. Retrieved on June 17, 2005, from www.pcaobus.org/Inspections/ Statement_Concerning_Inspection_Reports.pdf.

Public Company Accounting Reform and Investor Protection Act of 2002, S. 2673, 107th Congress. Retrieved on January 28, 2004, from http://thomas.loc.gov/cgi-bin/query/ z?c107:S.2673.

Public Company Accounting Reform and Investor Protection Act of 2002, H.R. 3763, 107th Congress, P.L. 107–204. Retrieved on January 28, 2004, from http://frwebgate.access .gpo.gov/cgi-bin/getdoc.cgi?dbname=107_cong_public_laws&docid=f:publ204.107.

Ramos, Michael. (2003). "Auditors' Responsibility for Fraud Detection." Adapted from Fraud Detection in a GAAS Audit–SAS 99 Implementation Guide. Retrieved on July 21, 2005, www.aicap.org/pubs/jofa/jan2003/ramos.htm.

Rappoport, Michael. (October 4, 2005). "Watchdogs Frustrated by Sarbanes Extension," CorpWatch, Down Jones Newswire.

Reddington, William C. (March 31, 2005). "D&O Underwriting Complications of Sarbanes-Oxley," American Re, http://www.amre.com/.

RevenueRecognition.com. (2005). "The Compliance Chasm." Retrieved on July 3, 2005, from www.softrax.com/pdf/ComplianceChasm_PPC2.pdf.

Securities and Exchange Commission v. HealthSouth Corporation and Richard M. Scrushy. (2003). Civil Action No.CV-03-J-0615-S. Retrieved on March 26, 2005, from www.sec.gov/litigation/complaints/comphealths.htm.

Securities and Exchange Commission v. Richard A. Causey, Jeffery K. Skilling, and Kenneth L. Lay. (2004). Retrieved on June 13, 2006, from http://fl1.findlaw.com/news .findlaw.com/hdocs/docs/enron/ussklng122805opn.pdf.

Securities and Exchange Commission v. Timothy A. DeSpain. (2005). Litigation Release No. 19067. Retrieved on June 17, 2005, from www.sec.gov/litigation/litreleases/lr19067 .htm.

Securities and Exchange Commission v. WorldCom. (2002). Civil Action (Securities Fraud). Retrieved on March 26, 2005, from www.sec.gov/litigation/complaints/complr17588.htm.

Securities and Exchange Commission v. Xerox Corporation. (2002). Civil Action No. 02–272789 (DLC). Retrieved on February 21, 2005, from www.sec.gov/litigation/complaints/ complr17465.htm.

Schein, Edgar. (1992). Organizational Culture and Leadership, 2nd ed. San Francisco: Jossey-Bass Publishers.

Shister, Neil. (October 2005). "Logistics Outsourcing Meets Sarbanes-Oxley," World Trade, vol. 18, no. 10, http://www.worldtrademag.com/CDA/Archives/483c170abaaf7010VgnVCM 100000f932a8c0

Sinclair, Matthew. (June 1, 2004). "Nonprofit Whistleblowers Need Protection," Nonprofit Times, http://nptimes.com/.

Skilling, Jeffrey, and Kenneth L. Lay. (2004). Litigation Release No. 18776. Retrieved on June 29, 2005, from www.sec.gov/litigation/litreleases/lr18776.htm.

SmartPros, LTD. (2005). "Investors Support Pre-Sox Rollback." Retrieved on July 2, 2005, from http://accounting.smartpros.com/x48762.xml.

Thorne, Jerry, R. David Mautz, Gwendolyn Highsmith-Quick, and Diana R. Robinson. (November/December 2004). "Recognizing Misleading Financial Statements: Lessons from SEC Enforcement Actions," Commercial Lending Review, http://www.commerciallendingreview .com/.

Tyler, J. Larry, and Errol L. Biggs. (March 2004). "Conflict of Interest: Strategies for Remaining 'Purer Than Caesar's Wife,'" Trustee, vol. 57, no. 3, p. 22.

Van Orden, Jim. (September/October 2004). "The Cost of Compliance: How Small Businesses Can Tackle Sarbanes-Oxley," AFP Exchange, vol. 24, no. 5, http://www.itspa.net/pressroom/press_detail.asp?id=124.

Ventures, G. (2005). "For Entrepreneurs: Financial Controls for Start-Ups. Retrieved on June 30, 2005, from www.gaebler.com/Small-Business-Financial-Controls.htm.

Vishneski, John S. III. (December 1, 2003). "New Liabilities Created by Sarbanes-Oxley: Are Your Directors, Officers Covered?," National Underwriter, vol. 107, no. 48, p. 36.

Wilhide, Kathleen F., and Terrace DeWald. (May 2004). "Compliance and Technology: Lessons Learned in the Financial Services Sector." IDC/Kahn Conference Proceedings, San Jose, CA.

Index